Yatesy

'Rap!' goes Ol. 'Talk down the mike! That sounded *hard*!'

Everyone knows something good's going to happen. The sound tightens up. Yatesy seizes on to the mike. He squeezes it till his hand shakes. Then, suddenly, there's words. Bucketfuls of words, spilling out of Yatesy's mouth, bouncing off the walls.

This is a tense and gripping story about a school band. It had been Ol's idea to play the Christmas concert; his second idea was to get a band together, and a most extraordinary band it turned out to be. Half of them couldn't play, most of them didn't like each other, and none of them had ever been on a stage. Then Yatesy arrived, Yatesy with his reputation for being kicked out of several schools, for fighting . . .

As the day of the concert loomed nearer, it grew less and less likely that the band would be able to perform. But Ol couldn't afford to back down. He was determined that nothing would get in his way . . .

This is an exciting, up-to-date first novel by a new young writer, Jon Blake. His experiences of teaching drama and English in the roughest of secondary school environments has inspired him to write for his pupils. He lives in Essex.

+ Plus ▸

JON BLAKE
Yatesy's Rap

Penguin Books

PENGUIN BOOKS

Published by the Penguin Group
27 Wrights Lane, London W8 5TZ, England
Viking Penguin Inc., 40 West 23rd Street, New York, New York 10010, USA
Penguin Books Australia Ltd, Ringwood, Victoria, Australia
Penguin Books Canada Ltd, 2801 John Street, Markham, Ontario, Canada L3R 1B4
Penguin Books (NZ) Ltd, 182–190 Wairau Road, Auckland 10, New Zealand

Penguin Books Ltd, Registered Offices: Harmondsworth, Middlesex, England

First published by Viking Kestrel 1986
Published in Puffin Books 1988

Copyright © Jon Blake, 1986
All rights reserved

Made and printed in Great Britain by
Richard Clay Ltd, Bungay, Suffolk

Except in the United States of America,
this book is sold subect to the condition
that it shall not, by way of trade or otherwise,
be lent, re-sold, hired out, or otherwise circulated
without the publisher's prior consent in any form of
binding or cover other than that in which it is
published and without a similar condition
including this condition being imposed
on the subsequent purchaser

I'll say this for you, Miss Harris. You was the only teacher that ever give us a fair hearing. Come to that, you was the only *person* that ever give us a fair hearing. We never meant to drive you away, miss. All right, so there was the bullying, and the shoplifting, and the bomb hoax, and Olly's protection racket. But we was only *first years*, miss! Making little mistakes is all part of growing up, ain't it miss?

Anyhow, I ain't going to go on like it's some kind of school assembly or what. I just want to tell you a little story.

1

It all goes back to the first day of term. They sent in the heavy brigade to sort us all out. Hatton, his name was. People said he'd quit the SAS cos he thought it was too soft. That was just talk, though. He was just another teacher that hated kids.

First thing Hatton did was to split everyone up from their mates. Then he give us a dress check. What's That On Your Feet? he says to Iqbal. Dockers, says Ickie. That's Funny, says Hatton, I Thought Dockers Were People Who Worked In Docks.

God. This *was* going to be a long term.

I don't know if Hatton had relatives running a jumble sale or what. He had Kev's A-team vest off him, Angie's baseball cap, Gordon's parka, Azi's gauntlets, and Gail's necktie. Tell you miss, it's lucky the heating's been fixed. Mind you, Ol and me, we was *cruising* along so far. I'd got me jumper right way round, and as for Olly – well, he wasn't even wearing his rasta hat. Oh miss, Ol was such a good little boy. Ol was *reformed*.

Next, Hatton give us what he called his briefing. How Sir liked to do things, you know. Full of surprises, he was. For instance, he liked quiet. He liked order. And he *hated* complaints from other teachers about *bad behaviour* and *slovenly work* by his class.

We're in raptures, of course. But Ol's already at work. He's unloading these folders out of his bag, piles and piles of them. There's one marked English, one for Science, one for Women, one for just about everything under the sun. Pretty soon old Ol's disappeared behind them altogether.

'All right,' says Hatton. 'What's the game, Charlie?'

A gap opens up in the folders. Ol's face appears in the gap. 'Just wanted to make some notes, sir,' he says.

'Is that so?' says Hatton. 'I wonder what note your head would make if I hit it with a stick of chalk?'

Hatton gets his first laugh. It don't come from Ol.

The fightback wasn't long coming. Hatton was just telling us we was second years, and that meant acting grown-up. Except acting grown-up did not include answering back. And it certainly didn't mean talking out of turn like *someone was talking now*!

'Why is it,' says Hatton, 'that ever since I started speaking to this class, there has been a *constant babbling noise* right under my nose?'

'It's comin' from yer mouf, sir,' says Ol.

'Get up!' screams Hatton. Every arse in the room obeys him. But Ol's comes up furthest, with a little help from his new teacher.

'You are a wit, aren't you, Charlie?' says Hatton.

'Me name's Olly, sir.'

'I said, you are a wit, aren't you, Charlie?'

'Dunno, sir.'

'And what would you like to be . . . when you *grow up*?'

Ol's face sets hard. 'Me mum wants me to be a lawyer, sir,' he says.

'Ha!'

Ol's face sets harder. 'It's a good job, sir,' he says.

'I agree,' says Hatton. 'It's a very good job. And it's all the more pity you're going to disappoint her.'

'Dunno what yer mean, sir.'

'Not many funny men get to be lawyers, Charlie. Or teachers. Or doctors. Or anything. I've got velvet curtains in my house, Charlie. Do you know why?'

'Cover the windows, sir?'

'Because I put my head down, Charlie. I respected my teachers. And I didn't behave like a two-year-old. Now sit down and keep your *fatuous* comments for the playground.'

Ol drops into his seat, rubbing his neck. Hatton scours the class for more jokers. He don't find none.

Being as it was the first week, there was piles of notices. The main one was about the Christmas Show. Hatton said the Christmas Show was the school's advert to the world. In other words, all the fat cats were coming – the ones we're going to have to crawl round one day for a job. Hatton can't believe it when no one volunteers for nothing. I mean, what about the gym display? The choir? Humping props for the staff panto?

'What about you, Charlie?' says Hatton. 'I'm sure we could fit a *comedian* in somewhere.'

Ol ain't amused. But what do you know? Next second, his hand's in the air! 'Sir,' he says. 'I got a *group*, sir.'

Eh?

'I see,' says Hatton. 'And does this little troupe have a name?'

'The Mighty Three,' says Ol. 'When there's three of us, that is.'

'When there's three of you?'

'Sometimes there's four. Sometimes me mum joins in.'

Someone laughs. Hatton's eyes narrow. 'And who's the other two? Your gran and the dog?'

Ol hangs his head. 'Our dog's dead, sir,' he says.

Hatton's near-on sorry and all, but just snaps out of it. 'And this menagerie has performed in public, has it?' he says.

'Sure, sir,' says Ol. 'Blueses, mainly.'

'Blueses?'

'You know, sir – when you kick the old dears out, an' all the street comes round, boppin', an' smoochin', knockin' back the Red Stripe –'

'You do *what*?'

'Not *me*, sir! I'm makin' the music, ain't I?'

Hatton takes a good long look at Ol. Ol gives him a

good long look back. Then Hatton makes a note in his register, and the Mighty Three are booked.

That wasn't the last of this Christmas Show. We all got volunteered for something in the end. Hatton give us all names, and called me and Ben the Flowerpot Men. Case you don't know miss, Bill and Ben was these gorms made out of flowerpots that come on TV with this moron daisy called Weed. Everyone said Thomas should be called Weed, but Hatton wouldn't have it. He told us about a kid in his old school whose ears stuck out. Wingnut, everyone called him. The kid got upset, then got in fights about it, then it ended up with his old man coming into school, a big load of trouble in the papers, and the head teacher resigning.

'Thomas's ears stick out!' someone shouted.

Ever since then we've called him Wingnut.

There was no game of footy that break. I found Olly kicking the school instead.

'I'm leaving,' he says to me.

'Maybe you just wound 'im up the wrong way,' I go.

'Crap!' says Ol. 'I saw me file on his desk. He knows all about me and Dan's gang. He knows we threatened them kids for money. I'd had it before he even saw me!'

Wham! Ol slams his foot into the wall. I give it a little kick and all.

'Here,' says Ol. 'You wanna be in a group?'

'I knew you 'adn't got one! Why d'yer say it?'

'I wanted to get 'Atton back, didn't I?'

''Ow?'

'I wanted 'im to tell all the other teachers he'd got somefin' for the show, then look a prat when he 'adn't.'

'But it's you that's gonna look a prat!'

Ol rubs his head. Maybe he'd been having late nights or something. 'Here, can you play anyfin'?' he goes.

'I learnt a bit on recorder.'

Ol screws his face up, like he's in pain. *'Recorder?'* he goes. 'What's the use o' that?'

'It's what they give me! Ain't my fault. Anyhow, what can you play?'

'I'm learnin' guitar.'

'What sort you got? Electric?'

'Dunno yet. I'm gettin' it tomorrow.'

Starting to get the picture miss? I was.

'You can play drums, or somefin',' Ol goes. 'Somefin' easy.'

'Cheers.'

'Well look keen, or somefin'! What's the matter wiv yer? Don't yer wanna do *nuffin'*?'

'Yeah . . . just, I promised me dad I'd work harder this term.'

Ol gives the wall a break, and squares up to me instead. 'D'you do everyfin' your ole man tells yer?' he goes.

'Well . . . yeah.'

'Hah!' Ol aims a kick at me. I jump back. Next thing I know, his hand's on me shoulder.

'Listen, Bill,' he goes. 'We *can't* back down now. We got to do that concert. Tell you what – I'll meet you after school tomorrow, and we'll go down the music shop. All right?'

'Er . . .'

'Cheers, Bill. You're a great bloke.'

Oh well, miss. It was no good me making out I wouldn't go. But I hadn't signed no contract with Olly, and if I had any sense I never would.

I've given you all the bad news first, so here's the good stuff. This'll kill you, miss. Guess who they give us for Drama last period? Dreamy Reaney! Remember him, miss? Him with the goaty beard and the Jesus sandals? What lines up behind the first years at dinner? Any lesson with him was going to be an ace doss, for sure.

Poor bloke. He was trying his best to make out he'd got strict over the holidays. Even had us in a straight line outside the Drama studio, and laid down the law: always take your shoes off before walking on the floor. Wait for his instructions. And *never in any circumstances* go up on the catwalk, which was *twelve foot high*, and only for teachers and caretakers. Not that we would, of course. We were a class of responsible young adults, weren't we?

Ah well. Good try, Dreamy.

'Right,' he says. 'Now, I want two volunteers to –'
'Me, sir!'
'Me!'
'Me!'
'WAIT!'

Reaney waves his arms about like a windmill gone mad till everyone shuts up and lets go of his jacket. He picks Gail and Jackie. Thinks he'll be safer with a pair of girls, he does. He tells them to start acting out any scene they like. In a moment he's going to join in, he says. Whatever character he turns into, they got to fit him in to the scene.

Gail and Jackie pretend they're in a kitchen. Jackie's a ratcatcher and Gail's a rat. Gail starts off by making them both some toast. Then she gets her paw stuck in the toaster.

That Reaney's a really weird bloke. He gets up, and starts tapping away on thin air, making a clucking sound. Then he shouts 'Hello! Anyone at home?' The girls look round.

'Good afternoon,' says Reaney. 'I am Doctor Watts.'

Jackie eyes him up and down. 'No you ain't!' she goes. 'You're Mr Reaney!'

'I'm afraid you are mistaken,' says Reaney. 'Look – here is my stethoscope.'

Reaney holds out a biro. Jackie takes it. 'That's a *biro*, sir,' she goes. 'You all right, sir?'

Reaney starts to panic. 'Let me in!' he goes. 'A patient needs examining!'

Gail walks across. She leans against Reaney, and drapes her arm round his neck.

'Oo, *sir*!' she goes. 'You gonna examine me, then?'

That does it. Reaney goes to pieces, and the class goes berserk. Scrapping, screaming, out the doors, up the walls. Would've been all right if Ickie hadn't gone too far and climbed the stairs up to the catwalk. Soon as Reaney saw him, his mouth started opening and closing faster than Tesco's doors on a Saturday. You couldn't hear him, of course, but bit by bit we all got the message. No one wanted to get reported to Hatton.

'I'm . . . I'm sorry I had to shout at you,' says Reaney. 'But I've *told* you about the catwalk, and –'

'Play's are *bòrin'*, sir,' says Angie. 'Can't we play stuck-in-the-mud?'

'Yeah!'

'Yeah, sir!'

'Stuck-in-the-mud, sir!'

This man will never make a teacher, miss. He gets so carried away shutting us up again, he clean forgets he's telling us off. 'Very well,' he says. 'But I shall be It.'

Bad decision, that. Especially when you run like Reaney does, like a floppy puppet with no sense of direction. In the end he settles for stretching his arms out like a signpost and herding some of the girls into a corner. There's no way out, except the door into the playground.

So that's where they go.

'Playground out of bounds, sir?' goes Ol. 'You should've said.'

Reaney bolts for it. The girls are halfway across the yard by now, with half the school hanging out the windows watching. That don't bother Dreamy, though. Flop, flop, flop after them he goes, bare feet and all.

Ol gets an idea. He tells Kev to get up on the catwalk, and grab that box full of curtains up there. Soon as Reaney's back outside the door, Kev's got to heave it over the edge. Then me and Ben's got to push it off out of sight. We'll find out why soon enough.

The girls arrive. Ol drops on his back like a sack of spuds. 'Now!' he shouts.

KER-RASH! That box must weigh a ton. We shove it off under a table, just as Reaney smashes through the door. 'What was that?' he screams, eyes like ping-pong balls.

Dead silence. Kev sneaks down, and the rest of us creep back against the walls. Ol's left on his own, stretched out on the floor, twitching.

'Fell off the catwalk, sir,' he whimpers.

Reaney drops into a chair. 'Oh my God,' he goes.

'Oh my God,' he goes again.

Kev edges towards Ol, inspects him, then turns to Reaney.

'Will you get in trouble, sir?' he goes.

Reaney puts a hand over his face. 'Get the nurse, will you?' he says to Kev.

'No sir,' goes Kev.

'No? What do you mean, no?'

'I don't like Olly, sir.'

'Can we get on wiv the game now, sir?' goes Gail.

Reaney's speechless. It's all he can do to lift an arm and point at Olly. 'Don't be stupid, sir,' goes Gail. 'Oliver can't be on, can 'e? Not wiv a broken neck. Let's 'ave Wingnut!'

'Yeah!'

'Yeah! Wingnut!'

Fat Bri takes off the neck-lock and sets Wingnut loose. Off he goes, with his teddy bear legs and his boss-eyes and his ears flapping in the wind. The rest of us are chasing round like a buffalo stampede. Meanwhile Reaney sits in the middle of it all with his mouth open, and Olly just lies and stares.

It don't take long for Wingnut to get frustrated. He's swinging out at everything – even the jackets on the coatpegs. The more he does it, the more the rest laugh, and the more they laugh, the worse he gets. He aims this massive kick at Jackie's leg, and his foot comes down CRUNCH . . . right on Olly's arm.

I don't know who come up furthest, miss – Ol or Reaney. But while Dreamy falls on his back, Ol falls on Wingnut. He lays into him like he's no more than a punchbag. Takes five of us to drag him off – arms still swinging.

Wingnut's curled up on the floor, dead still and quiet. His face is all swollen and purple, and sort of confused. Then a big wet tear plops out his eyes, runs down his cheek, and drips on the floor.

And that's why Wingnut likes strict teachers.

There's one thing I got to mention, miss, before I talk about our visit to the music shop. By lunchtime on the first day, rumour had got round that the new kid in 2r had got expelled from Canning Comp. You know what Canning's like, miss. So what did you have to do to get kicked out of there? Some people said he'd smacked the Head. Others said he'd stole the school bus. You know what it's like with rumours, miss. Remember when half the school thought Wingnut was county hang-gliding champion?

I saw this new kid twice on the first day – before and after the scrap. First time I saw him, he was leaning on that old ruin that used to be the scout hut. Honest miss, it wasn't human. Its hair was like straw. Its face was all dry, and cakey, and white, with cagey eyes, like an old dog's. Its neck was all stretched and wrinkly, like our tortoise's. And out of its sleeves come these two scaley hands, like birds' claws. One had a compass in it. The other was covered in scratches.

It wasn't long before some thirdies come up and had a go at it. It scurried off on its spindly legs to some other hiding-place. The thirdies laughed. They knew it couldn't hide for ever, not round school.

They were right. Just after four, me and Ol were round the bike sheds, pumping our tyres back up. There was this big racket down near the tennis courts, so we bombed over. McAdam was there, in his track suit, between the new kid and Dan – Dan from Ol's old gang that is. The new kid had blood over its mouth. Dan was looming over it, like a big black zombie, and picking at a rip on his elbow.

McAdam was mad. Give Dan a right mouthful he did, and told him he was out the football team that Saturday. Then he turned to the new kid, and come over all slow and heavy. You're on trial at this school, he says. We're watching you. At *this* school, he says, everyone is treated as an equal, no matter where they come from. We're all alike under the skin, he says, and don't you forget it.

Bloody hell, says Ol to me, I hope I ain't nothing like McAdam under *my* skin.

There wasn't a flicker on the new kid's face. Not even when McAdam said he'd be going on report. All it wanted to hear was the word to get lost. And when it come, it snatched its bag and turned like lightning.

Smack! Straight into me.

That put me out a bit, that did. Not cos it hurt or nothing, but cos of that manky claw it pushed me off with. It was *warm*, miss. Well, suppose it had to be really – but somehow I wasn't expecting it.

Soon as McAdam had revved up his racing bike and got lost, Ol asked Dan what it was all about.

'You'll hear about it,' says Dan. 'When that Yatesy squawks.'

2

I'm sure you ain't forgot where I come in Music last year, Miss Harris. Bottom. Joint bottom, in fact, with them fifteen others that refused to go ting-ting on the triangle and sing 'Lord Of The Dance' while Wally Whymark conducted us with a T-square. The only decent music lesson we ever had was when Ol come in that massive overcoat and pretended to play the piano. Wally was dead impressed till he noticed Ol's hands were white, and found out Wingnut was in the overcoat and all.

I don't mean to be cruel miss, but you get one crap teacher like Wally and it puts you off a subject for life. You just have to look at a piano and you think No Way. So when it come to Jim Jackson's shop window, I was near-on in a state of panic. All that gear! And how come one guitar's fifty quid and another's five hundred, when they look exactly the same?

Lucky Ol was with me. Nothing freaked him out. He told me all about the guitars, like the one what was all beat up being a starter's guitar, and the one with two necks being all right for his mum, cos everyone thought she'd got two pair of hands.

Seemed to me we might as well jump in the deep end and give some a try. Seemed to Ol we ought to wait a while.

'How much money you got?' I says to him.

'None of your business,' says Ol.

Seemed to me the shop'd be closing pretty soon. 'All right,' says Ol. '*You* go in an' try 'em out.'

You know miss, a lot of people might've thought old Ol was *scared* of going in that shop, less they knew what an expert on music he was. He had one last look at one window, then one last look at the other, then one last look at the 59 bus going by, then had a bit of problem with his laces. Meanwhile I was in danger of being late for tea, and I knew well enough what *that* meant. So guess who ended up going first?

I opened that door like a safecracker. Gently, gently...

DING! DING! DING!

A pair of yellow eyes spring up in front of me. I look to one side – music books, everywhere. I look to the other – a row of saxes, with great slithery mouths, all gaping at me. I feel back for the door.

'Oy! Get off!'

I think I felt Ol instead.

'What d'you want?' says the old guy in front of me, frowning.

'Just looking.' I squeeze past. I can feel them yellow eyes on me, all the way. More bloody kids with no money, that's what he's thinking. More trouble.

We're in this jumbly room, with guitars round the walls. They're all going What You Staring At, Mate? *You* don't know how to play me! There's cases too, and speakers, and a warm electrical smell, and all sorts of *weird* things put there just to confuse me. Thank God there's only one other customer, and he's sat with his back to us, trying out some guitar. Dead good it sounds. Absolutely *brilliant* in fact, the kind of playing I'd never do in a million years.

'I can do that tune,' says Ol.

Trying to make the best of it, I creep over to the wall and stare up at the nearest guitar. 'That one looks all right,' I go.

'Nah,' says Ol. 'Look for Strattercasters.'

'How'll I know one?' I go.

'Idiot,' says Ol. 'It says Strattercaster on them.'

'How's it spelt?' I go.

'S . . . t . . . Look, just get on and find one, will yer?'

We have a good hunt round for these Strattercasters, but it seems to be a bad day for them.

'Rubbish shop,' says Ol, just loud enough for the gaffer to hear. ''Ere – try that one instead.' Ol points to the nearest guitar, and shoves me towards it.

'You try it,' I go.

'You chicken?'

'You try it if you're buyin' it.'

Ol settles the problem his usual way. Whips his fist

under me nose like he's going to smack me one. I jump back, trip up, and fall straight over the bloke in the corner. The bloke drops his guitar, gasps, and shrivels up like a hedgehog. Next thing we know, the gaffer's there.

'All right – now get out of here!'

You'll never believe this, miss. Just as we're ready to crawl away, the hedgehog uncurls itself. It's wearing old Reaney's face!

'Come on!' says the gaffer. 'I said out!'

'No, please,' says Reaney. 'I know these lads. They're quite harmless.'

How Reaney could say that after our lesson with him I don't know. But know what, miss – he really stuck up for us. Even when the gaffer said our school turned out nothing but layabouts and vandals, and all the teachers should be shot.

'Sorry, sir,' I says, when the gaffer's left off.

'Doesn't matter,' says Reaney, picking up the guitar again.

'D'yer play guitar then, sir?' I go.

Ol elbows me. 'Course he does, stupid,' he says.

Old Reaney was as awkward out of school as he was in it. He started talking to us, but dead fast and quiet, with his eyes fixed on his guitar. 'I didn't know you boys were musicians,' he says to me.

'We didn't know you were, sir,' I go. 'Are you in a group?'

'Oh yes. Although we're off the road at the moment.'

'*Really*? What is it, sir? Funk?'

'Well, I don't like labels . . . jazz-rock, I suppose.'

'You gonna be on Top of the Pops, sir?'

'I very much doubt it. We're quite happy playing locally.'

'What you wanna be a teacher for, if you're in a group, sir?'

'Well . . . I can't make a *living* out of being in a group. I've got to eat, like the rest of you. Besides . . . I do actually *want* to be a teacher. It's much more important than most *pop music*.'

Olly looks blank. Who is this idiot here?

'We got a group,' he blurts out. 'We're looking for gear.'

There ain't a back exit out of this shop, is there?

'Ah,' says Reaney. 'And have you seen anything that interests you?'

'One o' them two,' says Ol, waving his arm at the nearest guitars.

'Oh,' says Reaney. 'It's a *bass* guitar you're after, is it?'

Ol looks at me. What's he want me to say? I shrug, and look away.

'I'm thinkin' o' gettin' one of each,' he says.

'A bass guitar *and* a lead?'

'You need a lead to plug it in, don't yer?'

'No! No! I mean lead *guitar*.'

'I know what yer mean!'

Reaney shakes his head. He stretches up, takes down

one of the guitars, and looks down it like a telescope. When he's finished, Ol picks it up and does the same. 'Looks OK to me,' he says.

'Do you think so?' says Reaney. 'I'd say it was rather warped.'

'Apart from that, yeah.'

Reaney's eyes flash up and look at Ol for the first time.

'You've got an *amp*, have you, Olly?' he says.

'A what?'

'An amplifier. To plug the guitar in to.'

'Oh, I don't bovver with that. I plug straight in.'

'Straight in? Straight in to what?'

'To the mains, of course.'

He'd blown it.

'Why don't you sit down a moment?' says Reaney. 'I've got some time.'

Ol and me settle on a speaker, and Reaney lays his guitar flat across his knees. He tells us about tuning, and pick-ups, and machine heads, and jack-to-jack leads, on and on and *on* till our heads are going round like catherine wheels.

'Hold on! Hold on!' says Ol. 'What you tellin' us all this for.'

'These are things you need to know,' says Reaney.

'I know all *that*!'

'Oh . . . I'm very sorry,' says Reaney. 'I was just going to tell you about p.a. rigs. You know about them as well, do you?'

'Oh yeah,' says Ol. 'But we don't bovver wiv 'em.'

'Don't bother with them? Well what do your vocals come through?'

'Well, *personally*,' says Ol, '*my* vocals come through me mouth.'

I'm starting to feel dead glad I left all the talking to Olly. Everything he says just seems to *stun* old Reaney. Rubbing his head, Reaney stands up and slopes off over the other side of the shop to take his guitar back. I grab Ol's arm. 'Listen!' I whisper to him. 'He can tell we don't know nuffin'! Why don't we just admit it an' get 'im to 'elp us?'

Olly huffs. But when Reaney comes back, Ol tells him he's found some gear he's never seen before, and could do with some advice on it. Reaney says he'll be glad to help, and glad to help us learn to play as well, if we like. Ol tells Reaney that he'll be all right, but I could do with some help, so thanks.

'By the way,' says Reaney. 'What do you call yourselves?'

'Judah Lions,' says Ol.

'That's odd,' says Reaney. 'It was the Mighty Three yesterday, wasn't it?'

He knew! He knew all along!

'Don't let on, will yer, sir?' says Ol, suddenly changing his tune.

'Don't worry about that. But you'd better get practising, hadn't you?'

Ol nods.

'Got to get the gear first,' I remind him.

Ol nods again, but he don't make no move. We stand there, waiting for something to happen, like a right bunch of idiots.

'Right,' says Reaney.

'Right,' says Ol.

'Er – did you want any help?' says Reaney.

'Em – did we?' Ol asks me.

My teatime's getting nearer by the second. I take Ol to one side.

''Ere,' I go. ''Ow much cash you got on yer, anyhow?'

Ol checks to make sure Reaney ain't watching, then opens out his trouser pocket.

Maths ain't really my subject, but a quick reckoning makes it out at something like 50p.

'I'll get a paper round,' says Ol.

I had to bring him down to earth somehow. All that gear we needed was going to cost hundreds and hundreds of pounds, and even if both of us did paper rounds, we'd still be sixty-five before we could afford it. Leave alone learning to play it, finding somewhere to practise, getting other people to play with, and working out how to write songs.

But you know what Ol's like, miss. You point these

things out to him, and his eyes are all over the place. He ain't listening. 'School should buy it for us,' he says.

'Yeah, but they ain't gonna, are they?'

'Look at the money they spend on books! An' the choir goin' to Finland!'

'Ol, they ain't *gonna* give us nuffin'!'

'I got it. I'll tell 'em I'll do wivout the books, if they'll get me a guitar instead.'

'Ol, we're just gonna make idiots of ourselves. Why don't you just tell Hatton the band's split up?'

'Look, shut up, will yer, Bill? You're like a bloody old moanin' granny! We're *playin'*, all right? Even if I got to use *our old cat for bagpipes* and *your arse for a bass drum*!'

The rumours about the new kid were growing, and none of them were making him sound no more lovable. Word had got round that before he'd got kicked out of Canning, he'd got kicked out of Ryan Park and all. Back at Ryan, he'd been in all these scraps with black kids. That must've been what Dan was on about. If this Yatesy was going to take on any of that crowd, he was in for a hard time.

The next time I saw him was when Hatton sent me to 2r with a message. They was in the English block, all copying off the board. 'There' and 'their', you know, like we do every year. Miss Lane had me waiting around like a prat while she patrolled the rows watching the criminals. Yatesy was right at the front, set on his own like a leper colony. His head was bent right down, and his pen was working so heavy and slow over the paper he might've been carving stone.

'Can I assume that everybody has finished?' says Miss Lane.

Yatesy carves on. Miss Lane homes in. Someone groans. Miss Lane leans right over, watching him, and tutting.

'Come on, Yatesy!' someone goes.

Miss Lane's head snaps up. 'Who was that?' she goes.

Watching Yatesy reminded me of them dreams when you're trying to run away, and your feet are glued down, and you're fighting and fighting and *fighting* to move, and it just won't happen. His book was a mess. For all that effort, his letters weren't even joined up.

Miss Lane leans over again, closer still. 'No! No! No!' she goes.

Yatesy's pen stops.

'What have I just said, Martin? "Their" meaning "belonging to them", spelt t,h,e,i,r! T,h,e,i,r! And how do we remember?'

Yatesy looks up to her.

'The answer isn't written on my face, Martin! I've just *told* you how to do it! On the board, Martin! What are the last four letters?'

Yatesy turns to the board, but he can't seem to see it.

'For God's sake! H,e,i,r! And what is an "heir", Martin?'

'Please, miss . . .'

'Yes?'

'It's like a rabbit, miss.'

Bedlam. Howls of laughter, rattling chairs, shouts of 'Yate-sy' in moron voices. Miss Lane tries to settle it, but it carries on, like a load of braying donkeys, for ages. When it finally quietens down, Yatesy's eyes are closed. Miss Lane turns to me, with that Am I Fed Up look teachers put on. 'Well? What is it you have to tell me?'

'Er . . . er . . .'

'Yes?'

'I forgot, miss.'

That Friday, Olly invited me over to his house. He'd had a grin on him all day, and I just knew something was up. Wouldn't let on though, would he? Said he just needed some help neutering his cat.

Halfway over to Churchill Street, Ol stops me in me tracks and tells me to listen.

'Why?' I go. 'What you gonna do?'

'Not me, you idiot! The 'ouse!'

We're outside a semi-detached with a lean-to garage. I strain me ears. Sounds like someone's battering something to death in there. 'Maybe they're demolishin' it,' I go.

'What, from the inside?'

I listen again. I realize the noise is in a rhythm. It's a drum kit!

'Wah!' says Ol. 'Listen to them rolls!'

'It's in the garage,' I go. 'Ey, let's 'ave a look in!'

Ol backs away. 'Get off,' he says. 'You don't know what lives in some o' these houses.'

'No 'arm in tryin'.'

Too late. He's gone. I got to run to catch him.

'Wait!' I go, grabbing for his bag. ''E'll be great in your band, won't 'e?'

Ol marches on. 'Probably a pro,' he says. 'We may be good, but we ain't good enough for one of *them* yet.'

We hit Churchill Street. 'Shanty Town', Ol calls it. Ain't nothing to what my old man calls it. Mind you, it looks all right to me. Good laugh, in fact. All the houses are painted with decent bright colours for a change, and everything that should've been going on inside was going on outside. Mums were bawling at their kids, kids were playing their stereos, and there was this couple snogging on a wall.

'Ain't you 'ad enough for tea?' Ol says to them.

We go into one of these little terraces. Ol's got these two little brothers that look identical. One tackles me down, and the other twists me neck off.

'Quit muckin' about, twinnies!' goes Ol. 'Where's mum?'

'Out.'

'C'mon, Bill – let's move.'

Ol yanks me free, and we race up the stairs. Ol barges through a door marked King Kong, and I follow.

Pwoh! Dirty socks!

'Bloody 'ell!' I go, holding me nose.

'Can't smell nuffin',' says Ol, looking hurt.

I look round. I guess this must be Ol's bedroom, although you can't actually see the bed, under all his clothes and magazines. Or the floor, which is carpeted in old records and tennis balls. Or the walls, which are plastered in posters of football teams and Bob Marley. I *could* make out a dressing table, but that was under about thirty mugs and a teapot in a rasta hat.

Now I know what the inside of Ol's brain must be like.

'Where's this cat then?' I go.

Ol reaches under the bed. Out comes this long flat black box. If the cat was in there, it must've got run over by a steamroller. Ol heaves the box on to the bed, and clicks open the locks on the side. I start to say something, and he holds up his finger. Watching me eyes, he ever-so-slowly lifts up the lid.

It's a guitar.

'Wah!' I go. 'Where d'yer nick that from?'

'Ssh!' goes Ol. He pulls out the guitar. After a bit of a struggle, he gets it on to his knees. It's one of them bass guitars, a black and white one. Just *brilliant*, it looks.

'Like me guitar then?' says Ol.

'Come on!' I go. 'You ain't bought that. Where d'yer nick it from?'

Ol picks at the strings, all cool, like he's been doing it all his life. Would've looked better if the guitar wasn't bigger than he was.

'Let me see,' he says. 'I fink I need me string-picker. Open me wardrobe, will yer Bill?'

I turn to Ol's wardrobe, grab the handle, and pull.

Oh no, miss. No. Oh no.

'What's the matter, Bill?'

I stand, and I stare, and I see it, but I still don't believe it. He's done a whole music shop! That wardrobe is *packed*, from the floor to the ceiling – amps, speakers, mikes, everything!

'Now come on, Bill. I've asked you for me string-picker.'

'I'm gettin' out of 'ere!'

''Ang on! Cool it, will yer?'

'Where d'yer get it, Olly?'

Ol looks down at his guitar, and strokes the back of his hand along the strings.

'Reaney give it me,' he says.

I sit down. This is going to take some working out. Did our Drama teacher need mental treatment? *'Why?'* I go.

'Says we deserve a fair chance.'

'Us? Why us?'

Ol shrugs.

'It ain't right,' I go.

'Eh? Why not?'

'You should earn what you get. My dad says you shouldn't take 'andouts, not off no one.'

Ol smacks the guitar and stares at me, with his eyes all flaming. 'If your old man's so bloody clever,' he goes, 'how come you live in a *pissy little flat* on the tenth floor? And how come your family's all so bloody miserable? And how come he keeps losin' money on the 'orses? Well? Come on, Bill!'

'Anyhow,' I go. 'We still ain't got no band.'

Ol smiles. He fishes in his pocket, pulls out a wad of papers, and hands the top one to me. 'Goin' round the music shops tomorrow,' he says.

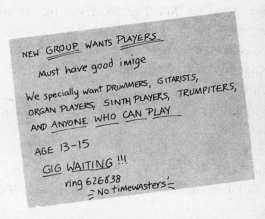

'All right?' says Ol. 'And in the meantime, I'm gonna learn 'ow to tune up, and all me notes, and I'm gonna practise after school every day, and all weekend, and right through the 'olidays, until I'm the best bass guitar player in England. Now, what's your next question?'

''Ere,' I go. ' 'Ow come you knew my old man lost on the 'orses?'

'It was a guess,' says Ol. 'Why, does 'e?'

Miss Harris, what can you do?

You probably been wondering why I've been going on about this new kid, Yatesy. Well now you're going to find out.

We walked into our tutor room on Monday morning and found Wingnut pinned up against the wall, with a big crowd of people round him. The new kid's sat by the sink, keeping his distance and being ignored for once. 'C'mon, Wingnut!' they're all going. 'Truth dare kiss or promise?'

Wingnut does a weak little smile, and tries to sound smart. 'Pass,' he says.

'Kiss!' someone yells. 'He said "kiss", everybody! Who d'yer wanna kiss then, Wingnut?'

Wingnut struggles. 'I'm not kissing anybody!' he squeals.

'You don' 'ave to kiss 'er body,' says Ickie. 'Only 'er face!'

Needless to say, Ol's got to get in on the act. He grabs Karen's alice band, and wiggles his way over to Wingnut. 'Darling!' he goes. 'Kiss me, darling!'

Wingnut's terrified. 'No!' he screams. 'Leave me alone!'

Ol creases up. Then someone else puts his oar in.

'Why don't yer leave off him?'

Silence. The new kid has spoken!

Ol straightens himself, pulls off the alice band, and squares up. 'Who banged your dish?' he goes.

Yatesy stands his ground. 'Don't need permission to speak, do I?' he says.

The crowd moves round behind Olly.

'You do in this school,' says Ol.

'It's a rubbish school, then,' says Yatesy.

Ol grabs for Yatesy's collar, then changes his mind. 'Don't want to catch nuffin', do I?' he says.

You can just *feel* that crowd urging Olly on. They been waiting for this.

'*I* know,' says Ol, with a smile creeping onto his face. 'Seeing as you're so bovvered about little Wingers 'ere, *you* can do 'is dare!'

Sound idea! Suggestions come flying in – let down Hatton's tyres, play chicken over the Bypass Road, just about anything and everything. But the one idea *everyone* goes for is that Yatesy's got to get up on the table – and sing a hymn!

'Anyone know any hymns?' says Ol.

We have a long think.

'Jerusalem!' says Kev. 'That's a hymn, ain't it?'

Yatesy don't make a fight of it. Couldn't really, could

he? No, he gets up on that table like a little lamb, and stands there waiting for the laughter.

'Let's 'ave a big 'and for the man wiv the golden voice,' says Olly. 'Elvis Yatesy!'

Everyone cheers, and Ol sticks a biro under Yatesy's mouth for a mike. 'Come on, Elvis! Your fans are waitin' for yer!'

Yatesy lifts his eyes. His fans are grinning their heads off. A few more arrive at the door, and a bunch of fifth years gawp in through the window.

Yatesy's head drops. His breathing seems to get slower and slower, like his batteries are gone. Then, all of a sudden, this kind of quiver goes through him. He snaps back his head, swallows hard, and ...

... God! He *can* sing! He's wicked!

You should've seen them faces change, miss. They were *turned to stone*, them fans of Yatesy's. He sung out just like a bird, staring through the crowd and the desks and the walls like he had X-ray eyes. He was possessed. I mean it, miss – this voice was just coming and coming like it was nothing to do with him, like his scraggy little body was being *used*. If he'd done just one bum note, or forgot one little word, we could've relaxed. But there was no way he was going to, not for a moment.

When it was over, there was a little pause. Then Yatesy climbed down, picked up his bag, and headed for the door. The crowd peeled apart before him. No jeering, no clapping, nothing. Just a feeling the game was over.

I slide over to Ol. 'You thinkin' what I'm thinkin'?' I ask him.

'What's that, then?'

'We need a singer.'

Ol shakes his head. 'No way, man,' he goes. 'Anyone can sing that old rubbish. We're doin' modern stuff.'

'Get on – he can sing that!'

Ol twists his biro about in his fingers.

'Why not, Ol?' I go. 'Who else is there?'

Next thing I know, the biro's flying across the room.

'We can't 'ave 'im, can we?' says Ol. 'You wanna tell Dan an' them?'

3

Old Ol had meant it when he said he was going to practise, miss. There was no sign of him at the youfie, or the rec, or even the Wednesday disco. According to Hatton, there wasn't much sign of his homework, neither. Still, Ol reckoned the effort was definitely paying off. After a week, he was already as good as most of them on Top of the Pops. By the end of term, he'd be giving solo concerts at the Albert Hall. So he said.

I told him that unless we got our fingers out, he'd be doing a solo concert at the Christmas Show and all.

'That's where you're wrong,' says Ol. 'I got an answer to me advert.'

'Yeah? What's 'e like?'

'Dunno. His old man rung up for him.'

'Sounds like a real pro.'

'I 'ad to tell him we never took drugs, or ate live chickens, or nuffin'. So 'e says he'll send his kid round Friday.'

'That's tonight!'

'Yeah, come on. You're helpin' wiv the interview.'

'What 'bout me old man?'

'Don't worry. 'E's vanished up his own arsehole. It was on the news.'

Five past four, and we're on our way to Churchill Street again. Ol's explaining to me, in plenty of detail, how come he's such a natural musician. Then we see Gail off up ahead, and Ol tells me to slow down.

'Why?' I go.

'I don't want to be seen near Gail. She's a slag.'

'Why?'

'She two-timed Darren Harvey.'

'But she never went out wiv 'im!'

'She led 'im on. She let 'im carry 'er bag.'

'Gail's just like that, ain't she? She's friendly.'

'Listen – whose side you on? Darren's my mate!'

Always got to be on someone's side, ain't you miss?

'Hey! Where's she going?'

Gail's turning into a house. Not just *any* house. The house we heard the drumming from, we're sure of it.

We had to get to the bottom of this. That's to say, *I* had to get to the bottom of it, while Ol hid up behind the garden wall. 'What shall I say?' I go.

'Complain about the noise.'

Ol dashes out, raps on the door, and dashes back again. The door opens, and I'm suddenly faced by Medallion Man.

'Yeah?'

I'm blinded by the hardware. This bloke must have half a scrap yard round his neck.

'I'm afraid I've come to . . . see Gail.'

Medallion Man leans back, opens his trap, and yells at the top of his voice. 'Sis! It's your boyfriend!'

Next thing I know, there's half the family in the hallway. Mother, father, little brother, granny, pet poodle, you name it. All yapping and gawping and fighting for a ringside seat. Miss, I died.

'Oh – it's only *Flowerpot*.'

Gail pushes her way through. Medallion Man grins at her. 'Don't go much on your taste, sis,' he says.

'You jokin'?' says Gail. 'I only go out wiv *men*.'

I stick me chest out six inches.

'For goodness sake!' says Gail's mum. 'Poor little mite! Let him in, will you?'

They let me in, and Gail's mum herds the tribe away. Just before the door closes, there's a scrambling sound behind me. Olly.

'Who's the drummer?' he says to Gail.

Gail gives him a black look, if you see what I mean.

'Looking for someone for your *group*?' she says.

'What you sayin' it like that for?'

'Oliver, everyone *knows* you ain't got one.'

Poor old Ol. Looks dead offended, he does. Didn't Gail know about the single we put out? Or the tour of Britain? Or the record contract we turned down? This girl just *did not read the papers*!

'Come on then, you two,' says Gail. 'I'll show yer the drummer.' She leads us through to the yard, and then the garage. All the inside's done out with egg boxes round the walls. And where the car should be, there's this old sparkly blue drum kit. We wander round it, tapping the cymbals and testing the foot pedals. Gail asks us if we've quite finished, and then sits herself behind it.

'Get off,' says Ol. '*You* ain't the drummer.'

'If you say so, Oliver.'

BADABADABADABADABADABADA *SMASH*!

'All right, so you can do a roll. That ain't what drummin's about. Drummin's about *beat*.'

'*Is* it, Oliver? Well thanks for tellin' me.'

SMASH! BUPPABUPPABUPPA SMASH! BUPPABUPPABUPPA

Strikes me Ol should keep his mouth shut. That Gail's been practising, no doubt about it. And can she make a racket! She must have a photo of Olly on each of them, the way she smacks them drums.

Gail's mum slides through the door and edges up next to us. Dead proud, she looks. 'Not bad, is she?' she says to Ol.

'*Eh?*' says Ol.

'I said, *not bad, is she?*'

'*Oliver,*' says Ol. '*Oliver Lester.*'

Gail's mum shakes her head and turns to me. '*We*

can't afford much, but when Gail's really got her heart set on something . . .'

'*Eh?*'

'I said, *we can't* . . . oh.'

Thank God. Gail's stopped. Her mum gives her a little round of applause, so I join in. Ol looks daggers at me.

'That hi-hat's coming on very well, darling,' says Gail's mum. 'Now don't forget to help daddy with the salad, will you?'

'Now don't forget to help *daddy* with the *salad*, darling,' says Ol, soon as Gail's mum's gone.

'What's the matter, Oliver?' says Gail. 'Somefing niggling you?'

'*You* can't drum,' says Ol.

'Says who?'

'Telling you. You can't drum,' says Ol, snatching out with his hand. 'I've got the sticks.'

I give Ol his guitar pick. He leans over his bass, gets his fingers right, then whacks the string, hard as he can, four times.

BARRM! BARRM! BARRM! BARRM!

All the mugs dance about on the dressing table.

'Great, eh?' goes Ol.

I ain't smiling.

'We ain't 'avin' 'er,' says Ol.

'Why *not?*'

'She's spoiled.'

'Spoiled? Why?'

'That kit must 'ave cost 'undreds. She never 'ad to *earn* it or nuffin', did she?'

'Come on, Ol! *You* wouldn't've turned it down!'

Ol fixes his fingers in another place, and blasts away again. 'Anyhow,' he goes. 'She's stroppy.'

'But she ain't, Ol. She's all right most of the time, unless you get 'er back up.'

'Fancy 'er, do yer?'

'No!'

'I still say she's stroppy. Anyhow . . .'

'Yeah?'

Ol reaches down and turns a machine head. 'She's a girl,' he says.

'Oh, *Ol*!'

'I ain't 'avin' a girl in the band! Girls are a pain in the arse. All they talk about is *boyfriends*, and *'aircuts*, an' knittin' a pair of feet for *Princess Di's new baby*.'

'Yeah, but Gail learns to drum an' you 'ate 'er even more! What's a girl got to do to be all right by you?'

Ol thinks about it. ''Ave a sex change,' he says.

I give up. Ol takes a swig out of a can of Coke, then gets back to proving what a great musician he is. Except, to be honest, it sounds bloody awful. 'Don't you know no tunes?' I asked him.

'You don't play tunes on a bass. You play *lines*, don't yer?'

'Go on – play a line then.'

'I *am* playin' a line!'

I listen hard. All I can hear is one note . . . then another note . . . then the first one again . . . then the second one again. 'You know all the notes now, do yer?' I ask him.

'Sure! This one's a *A*, an' this one's a . . . *B* . . . an' this one's a *A*. . . . an' . . . *this* one's . . . a *B*.'

Whatever I could hear had nothing to do with what was coming through to Ol. He was in seventh heaven. Got up on his feet he did, staggered round the room, shouted out Reggae! and then fell over backwards. I thought he'd never stop. He did right enough though, when that bedroom door come open.

'Oliver!'

'Mum!'

It's funny Ol ain't so big himself, cos his old lady plugged that doorway good as any door. I swear, if you stood her on her side, she wouldn't be no shorter. When she come marching in that room, Ol and me were near on jammed to the walls to stay clear.

Out of the socket comes Ol's plug, and out of his hands comes the bass guitar.

'And where ya gat dis fram?' she goes, in this great booming voice.

'It's mine, mum, honest!' goes Ol, cringing away.

'Don't you lie ta me!'

'Mister Reaney give it me, mum – cross me 'eart!'

'Who's dis Mistah Reaney? Why'd he give it ya?'

'Our Drama teacher, mum – 'e wants to 'elp us, God's truth 'e does, mum!'

Ol's mum turns on me, and near on gives me heart failure. 'Dis true?' she goes.

'Yes!' I squeak, backing into the cracks in the wall.

Ol's mum gives the guitar another once-over. Then the lead, and then the amp.

'Well,' she says. 'It's very nice. But you're nat gwan play it 'ere.'

'Oh mum! Why? Look, I just play it through this *tiny* amp. It don't make much noise.'

'It won't mek a lat o' noise in yar wardrobe, dat's fa sure!' Ol's mum grabs Ol's amp and carries it like a biscuit tin over towards the wardrobe.

'No, mum!' shouts Ol. 'Me dirty socks! They'll kill yer!'

Ol's mum don't exactly look the type to snuff it at the stink of dirty socks, even Ol's. She reaches for the handle, and yanks open the door.

Miss, if looks could kill, Olly would've been *very dead*.

'It's all right!' goes Ol. 'It's all right, mum – I'm gettin' a group togever!'

'Nat 'ere, y'are nat!' goes his mum. 'Ya'll 'ave us thrown out the 'ouse!'

I couldn't see no one throwing Ol's mum too far, to be honest. She just stood there, and she glared, and Ol shrivelled, and I got the feeling we'd be moving gear before too long.

There's a shout from downstairs.

'Mum! Someone at the door!'

'Don' give me "someone" – who is it?'

''E says 'e's come about the group, mum!'

'*'As* 'e indeed?'

Ol's mum marches off out, breathing fire, and thunders down the stairs. Ol looks at me with Panic Now writ all over his face. We chase off after her, but come to a dead halt downstairs in the hall. She's already at the door, and we can't see a thing past her. But whoever's out there can't be worse than Gail, says Olly, and *could be* . . . well, who knows? Someone who could actually *play*? Someone with an *image*? Someone cool as Olly, even?

Things don't look too bad. She ain't clocked him, or sat on him, or even give him earache. She's being dead polite, in fact. And after what seems half an hour, with us fighting for a glimpse, she finally says Come In.

All is revealed. There on the step, clutching a massive cardboard box, is Wingnut.

I could go into all the details of Wingnut's audition, but I wouldn't like to depress you, miss. Needless to say, it was the most embarrassing experience of my life. And Ol's, and Wingnut's. Mrs Lester took charge of the whole thing, and asked Wingnut if he could play 'A Nightingale Sang In Berkeley Square', then sang it all herself instead, till all three of us were that red you could boil kettles on our heads. Ol and me got told off for our stony faces, and sent out to the kitchen while Mrs Lester tried to get something out of Wingnut and his keyboard thingy. Soon as it was over, she told Ol she didn't much understand modern music, but being as Wingnut was so *polite*, we'd got to have him in the group. And when Ol started moaning, and saying what a prannet Wingnut was, and what a pathetic image the band'd have, it only made her more set on it.

I looked on the bright side. If Wingnut had sold his home computer to buy that keyboard thingy, he must've been *some* good on it. No good telling Ol that though. He was all for putting a new advert round, maybe trying the papers and all. Whatever happened, we weren't going to end up with a load of *kids from school*.

As for somewhere to practise, Ol'd got that one well under control. We were going round Reaney's house.

'You *sure*?'

'Course I'm sure! Reaney won't mind.'

'You know where 'e lives then?'

'Course I do! Picked it up from there, didn't we?'

'Wassit like, then? I never been in a teacher's house.'

'You ain't lived.'

Ol wasn't joking. Reaney lived on that new estate, all them council maisonettes. Looked normal enough outside, but once you got *in* – well, it was something else. Reaney never bothered none with carpets, or curtains, or furniture, or none of that normal boring stuff. Didn't bother much with air freshener, neither. But when it come to books, and boxes, and paper, and bits of guitar, old Reaney was world champion.

'Wah!' I says to him. ''Ave you read all them books, sir?'

'I suppose so,' he goes. 'At one time or another.'

'You must be a genius, sir!' I go.

'Please,' says Reaney. 'Call me Dunc when we're not at school.'

'Call you *what*?' goes Ol.

'Dunc.'

'Got a kettle, sir?' goes Ol. 'Dyin' for a coffee.'

'Yeah,' I go. 'Where's the kitchen, sir?'

Reaney comes over all awkward. 'We're in the kitchen,' he says.

Like I said, something else. This kitchen of Reaney's ain't got no fridge, no washer, and – till you move all the pots – no sink. Mind you, give him his due – there *is* a kettle, and a little camping stove he forks out the cupboard.

'God, sir,' goes Ol. 'Are you poor, or somefing?'

'Ol!' I go.

'No, no, it's fine,' says Reaney, and goes on and tells us *exactly* how much wages he gets a month! Honest miss, not even my big brother'd tell me that! Don't stop there, neither. He starts on about how teachers' wages depends on governments, and how some governments just don't care about most people, just the ones with

Rolls Royces and villas in the South of France. He asks us what we think about that, and Ol says he's going to make sure he gets himself a Rolls Royce and quick.

After coffee we got a guided tour of the rest of the house. There was a bathroom with washing in the bath, a living-room where the only thing living was crawling up the wall, and a bedroom with no bed – just a mattress on the floor. Tapes and books and smelly clothes all over the place.

'Pwoh!' says Ol. 'When d'yer change yer sheets last, sir? You could stand this lot against the wall!'

'You can talk,' I go.

'What you mean?' goes Ol. 'You could eat your dinner off my floor!'

'Yeah,' I go. 'Looks like you already did.'

That Reaney was awful slow on the uptake, miss. It really worried him as to why he'd got to stand his sheets against the wall. But we sort him out in the end, and get down to the real business why we come.

'You don't mind if our band comes round 'ere an' practises, do yer, sir?' says Olly.

Don't think Reaney was expecting that, somehow. 'Er . . . er . . . well, *no* – no, you can't,' he stammers.

'Eh? How come?'

'Well, this is an *estate* . . . there are people living all round here.'

'We won't charge 'em! They can listen free!'

'I'm sorry, it's out of the question.'

Ol sees he means it, and sinks into a sulk. But Reaney's thinking. After a bit, he nods his head and smiles. 'I think I may have the answer,' he says. 'The school has a small annexe which used to be used for the scouts. The Deputy Head was talking about possible uses for it just the other day. Perhaps if someone offered to clear it out, do it up a bit –'

'Got it, sir!' goes Olly. '*We* could do it up! Then use it to practise in!'

'Yes,' says Reaney. 'Yes, that was the idea. Of course, you'll have to clear it with Dr Dance first.'

'*No* problem,' says Ol. 'Disco's even softer than . . . some uvver teachers.'

'I'm sure he'll welcome the idea,' says Reaney. 'But in the meantime, I've no objection to *solo* practising at my house.'

Suddenly things are looking up again. We're that happy we invite ourselves to tea.

'I'm afraid I don't normally keep food,' says Reaney.

'We'll eat yer books then,' says Ol, racing off to the kitchen.

Half a minute later, Ol's back with two tins of beans and a packet of mash for ten, looking for an opener. Old Dreamy don't mind a bit! People've had their arms chopped off round my house for less than that!

You never knew I could cook, did you miss? Neither did I till then. But I boiled up the water all by meself, *and* poured it on the potato granules. *And* dropped in a lump of marge and stirred it all up. All Ol did was heat up the beans. He still made out he was head chef, seeing as he was cooking the *proteins*.

Any rate, it was an ace meal, and all the better for not having to sit at table. Or keep your mouth shut when you was eating. Mind you, after watching Ol rattling on with his gob bunged up with squidge, I started to understand why they invented that rule. 'Ain't you got no table manners?' I go.

'We ain't on the table, are we?' goes Ol. 'These are *floor* manners.'

I told Ol he was a pig, so next thing he's down on all fours and oinking. Then he comes rooting round for my beans, and I fight him off with me fork. He falls over backwards and sits on his dirty plate. Reaney and me near on piss ourselves laughing, but being as Olly's always got to be cool, he just stays sitting there, and makes out he likes it.

By the time we'd pushed all that stuff down, we never felt like moving for a week.

'Sir, you know this group,' I says to Reaney, after a bit. 'D'yer fink it's a good idea, then?'

'Of course. Everyone's got talent. They just have to discover it.'

'Ain't so sure about that, sir. My old man says me best bet's to work for me CSEs an' aim for an office job.'

'And what if you don't get one? What will you fall back on then, if you haven't got *interests*, and you haven't got *belief in yourself*? Jobs are getting fewer all the time.'

'I know, sir. Me old man says teachers are to blame.'

Reaney's face drops.

'No, no . . . not *just* teachers, sir. The unions and all.'

'*I'm* in a union,' says Reaney.

'Well . . . not *your* union, maybe.'

Think I'll shut up, miss.

'We're gonna be brilliant, ain't we, sir?' says Ol. 'We're gonna be on Top of the Pops, an' go round the world, an' get loads o' groupies, an' . . . an' . . .'

'And think you're really important,' says Reaney.

'Yeah, an' think we're dead important,' says Ol.

'When really you're just a bunch of spoiled, overpaid *brats* with nothing to say except how wonderful you are.'

'Yeah, when really . . . hang on.'

'I'm sorry, Olly . . . I'm not getting at you.'

Everything goes quiet, and I curse meself for spoiling everything and getting Reaney uptight. Don't take much to make friends again, though. I ask Reaney if he's got a dishwasher, and he asks me if I'm volunteering. Ol and me make a quick move, and it ain't towards the sink. We're only joking, though. Washing up ain't so bad with Ol there making up all these negro spirituals about working your fingers to the bone for Massa Reaney and all that.

Massa Reaney inspects the pots, and decides to free his slaves. Till school tomorrow, that is.

I got a rollicking off me dad as soon as I got home from Reaney's that night. They never liked me hanging round with Olly, seeing as he was a bit of a troublemaker, and a bit sarcy, and a bit black. I could've just jacked it in then, I suppose. Thing was though, I'd started talking about *our* band, and *our* gig, and *our* problems. Not that I made none of the decisions. I'd been all for trying Yatesy, then Gail, and now Wingnut. But first thing Monday morning, all Ol'd say was that he'd 'handle' Wingnut, seeing as he always knew the best way to 'handle' people. So there's Wingnut, sat down all happy with his book in the library, and next thing he knows he's in a neck-lock, fighting for his life.

'I got you on a Chinese pressure point, right?' says Ol. 'You do what you're told or you're dead inside a minute. Right?'

'Nnnngh.'

'You ain't tellin' no one 'bout Friday night, right?'

'Nnnngh.'

'An' you're ringing up my mum, right? You're tellin' 'er you're joinin' anuvver band. Right?'

'Nnnngh.'

'You better!'

Ol lets go. Then the waterworks start.

'You!' goes Wingnut. 'I'm tellin' *Dr Dance* on you!'

Crash! Over goes the chair, and off goes Wingnut on course for Disco's office.

Ol tries to smile it off. Then his face drops. *'Disco!'* he goes, and do we move.

It's too late. He's on his way in.

'After 'im!' goes Ol.

'No!'

No use. Ol skids into Disco's office after Wingnut, and like an idiot I follow. Disco's sat under the window, glasses cock-eyed, beaming his head off, and singing at Wingnut.

'Knock three times on the ceiling if you wa-ant me,
Twice on the pipe, if the answer is no-o-o.'

He sees us, and pushes a chair forward.

'Take a chair,' he says. 'But don't forget to bring it back!'

We give in! Cane us, just spare us the jokes!

'Now, gentlemen,' says Disco. 'What can I –'

Oh-oh. He's noticed Wingnut's face.

'Have you been crying, Thomas?' he says.

' 'E's upset, sir,' Ol blurts out.

'So I see,' says Disco. 'What I don't know is why.'

'They just –' blubs Wingnut.

'They just won't give us nowhere to practise, sir,' goes Ol. 'Wingers is upset cos our group can't practise, sir.'

'Ah!' says Disco, beaming up. 'The much awaited pop group! So Thomas is one of your number?'

Ol edges up close to Wingnut. ''E's our keyboards player,' he goes. ''E's brilliant. Probably best in the country.'

Do what?

"'E writes all the stuff,' Ol carries on. 'Does all the compostin'.'

'Composing,' says Disco.

'Compostin' *an'* composin',' says Ol.

Wingnut's taking a liking to this. He dries his eyes.

'The band's called Wingnut an' the Bolts, sir,' says Ol.

Wingnut smiles. He's bought it.

'That's wonderful!' says Disco. 'Wonderful. And who else makes up this *creative foray*?'

'Let's see,' goes Ol. 'There's me on bass, an' vocals, an' guitar ... an' Bill on recorder ... an' ... oh yeah – Gail on drums.'

Disco rocks right forward and near on falls all over us. 'Little Gail?' he goes. 'Gail from your class? Well, I am *delighted*. She's got that look about her, hasn't she?'

'Yeah,' says Ol, through his teeth.

'Sounds like another Honey and the Honeycombs,' says Disco.

'You what, sir?' goes Ol.

'Honey on the drums! You must remember! Let me see ...

> Walk right back! I just can't bear it!
> I've got some love and I long to share it!
> Walk right back, I'll show my love is tru-ue!'

'Yeah, yeah, we remember,' says Ol, before Disco can do his dance routine and all.

'*Tremendous* gimmick,' says Disco.

'Tremendous what, sir?' goes Ol.

'Gimmick! Goodness me, I thought you kids today knew all there was to know about pop music. Gimmick, like Sandie Shaw singing in her bare feet.'

'Oh, *I* know, what you mean, sir!' goes Ol. 'Yeah, our gimmick's Wingnut's ears. 'E plays 'is keyboard wiv 'em.'

'*Does* he now?' says Disco, all serious. He looks a bit more close at them great radar dishes growing out of Wingnut's head. A pair of shy little hands creep up and pin them back a bit.

'Anyway,' says Disco. 'How can I help?'

'You know that old annexe, sir?' says Ol. 'That ain't used for nuffin' now, is it?'

'That *isn't* used for *anything*,' says Disco, setting him right.

'That's what I thought,' says Ol. 'Sir – I know we're only second years and that, an' teachers don't fink much o' being in a group, an' I got a bad name last year, but if we put in loads o' work, an' cleared it out, an' done it up, an' if we promised it'd only be for a while, an' uvver people could use it . . . couldn't we practise there, sir? We promise we –'

'Seems an excellent idea,' says Disco.

'But *sir*! We wouldn't . . . eh?'

'It's just the kind of thing it ought to be used for.'

Ol's stuck for words. Don't think a teacher's ever agreed with him before.

'I'll have to clear it with the Head, of course. He'll probably think of ten thousand reasons why not. But I'm sure I can talk him round.'

'You're a pal, sir!' goes Ol, reaching into his pocket. ''Ere, 'ave a Polo, sir!'

'Thank you,' says Disco. He takes the Polo and files it away in his drawer. 'I must say, I *am* looking forward to seeing young Gail play those drums!'

The celebrations didn't last long. The moment we were back in the corridor, Ol dropped into a chair and stamped his foot. ''Ow we gonna 'ave a group wiv *Wingnut* in it?' he goes.

Wingnut's just about to sit next to Ol, but changes his mind. 'I don't want to play, anyhow,' he goes.

'We'll get laughed offstage,' says Ol.

'He says he don't wanna play, anyhow,' I go.

Ol stares up at Wingnut like he's got a screw loose. 'What you on about?' he goes. 'You're *playin'*. We ain't gonna lose that room now. We'll just hide you in a costume, or put you behind a screen, or somefing.'

Wingnut don't smile, but don't argue neither. For all this creeping round teachers, Olly's still his real hero.

'What 'bout Gail?' I go.

'Oh, no,' says Ol. 'That's anuvver matter. I'd rather *marry Hatton* than ask 'er to join the band.'

Have I told you about my eyesight problem yet, miss?

Must be getting worse. I was up in the Art room that dinner staring out the window, and I could've *swore* I saw Olly behind the bike sheds with Gail. I know it *couldn't* have been Olly, cos he was down on his knees, beating the ground in front of her. But when I opened the window, honest to God miss, it didn't half sound like him.

'All right! I take it back! You can drum, right?'

'Good as any boy?'

'Yeah, yeah. Good as anyone, 'ceptin' me.'

'Oliver . . .'

'Big deal! So you're as good as any boy!'

'Right. Now kiss my hand.'

'Kiss it yourself!'

'You wanna do the show?'

'I got mouth ulcers.'

'So what? I got septic fingers.'

The person that couldn't possibly be Olly checks around, pecks Gail's hand, then jumps up and wipes his mouth. Gail weighs him up. 'Well, I'll think about it,' she says.

'What?'

'Drummers're in big demand, y'know.'

Gail saunters off, back to the safety of her mates. That other person stands rooted to the spot, staring after her. He's completely lost for words.

No, that *definitely* couldn't be Olly.

I like work. No, I mean it miss, I really like it. I found that out soon as we started work on the annexe. With some help off Den, the caretaker, we learnt all about scraping and electric sanding, and painting and varnishing and even plastering. It was great, having something to *do*, something to *work towards*, stead of filling up folders with writing, and more writing, and diagrams of farming systems in the Middle Ages. We had a few *debates*, like, but in the main we was having a laugh. Even Wingnut pulled his weight. We got him on the school computer, working out how much paint and stuff we'd need. Then we got hold of these rollers and bright yellow paint, and started sending these great yellow roads round the walls, getting wider and wider till you couldn't imagine what a mess the room looked before.

Gets you talking, too, when you got something to do. Ol and me were just finishing off round the skirting board, when I asked him what we were going to do about shifting the gear.

'Winston,' says Ol.

'Who's Winston? Only Winston I know is Winston Churchill.'

'Yeah, that's him. Winston Churchill Lester.'

'I never knew you 'ad a bruvver.'

'I ain't. Not accordin' to me mum.'

'What you mean?'

'Winston's growed 'is locks. 'E's a rasta. 'E got kicked out o' school for readin' a bible in lessons.'

I touch in me last little spot, and set about cleaning me brush in the turps rag. 'What's 'e do now, then?' I go.

' 'E's in a group, ain't 'e? Seven Seals – they're doin' all right. 'E's savin' up to go back to Africa.'

'S'at where 'e comes from, then?'

'That's where we all come from, stupid.'

I put me brush away, and look for the paint lid. 'What you doin' 'ere, then?' I go.

'*You* brought us 'ere.'

'I never did!'

'You did! You 'it us over the 'ead and shipped us off to Jamaica. We was your *slaves*, man. We cut sugar cane for nuffin', so *you* could get rich, you thievin' git!'

'*I* ain't rich!'

'Then you says, "Come over to England! We need yer! Loads o' jobs 'ere!" So we come over. Then there ain't no jobs no more. So you says, "Go back to Jamaica! Stop takin' our jobs, you black bastards!" So *we* says, "All right. Just give us the money. We're off."'

I ram down the paint lid. Job done.

'I can't remember sayin' all this, Ol,' I go.

'S'all right,' says Ol. 'I forgived yer when yer lent me yer cassette last term.'

4

'No one can *hear* me!'

'What yer say, Wingnut?'

'I said no one can *hear* me!'

Ol switches off his bass. 'What yer shoutin' for?' he goes.

This was no good, miss, no good at all. Even with Winston's help, it's taken us near on an hour to shift the gear and set up. And ever since then, all we'd had was a lesson from Olly in playing A, G, F and E on the bass. I was sat there like a right prat next to a guitar I couldn't play, and Wingnut was slowly building up to a full-scale tantrum over the fact he never had a big amp like Ol's to play through.

As for *music* . . .

'Why don't yer play just a bit quieter, Ol?' I suggest to him.

'What you up to, anyhow?' goes Ol. 'You ain't even picked up the guitar yet!'

I take hold of it. I pick it up. I put it down again. '*I* don't know what to do wiv it!' I go.

'*Play* it!'

'I *can't*!'

Ol moves towards me, fists up. 'You play that guitar or I'll –'

Hang on. Someone's coming through the door. Backwards, Under a bass drum. ' 'Ow's it goin' then, boys?' says Gail.

No one moves, or says nothing. Gail struggles over the room fighting for breath, and dumps the drum. She's followed in by half her family, like an army of soldier ants, all carrying gear. I'm half expecting the poodle to wander through with a pair of cymbals strapped on.

'I thought you said she wasn't in?' I whisper to Ol.

Ol don't answer. He picks up his bass and plays with the controls, all self-conscious. Meanwhile, Gail's tribe wish us good luck and leave. Gail carries on sorting out, fixing together, and twisting away with her spanner. When she's done, she gets herself comfy, tests her foot pedals, and picks up the sticks.

'Playin' then, are yer?' mumbles Ol.

Gail looks at the sticks in her hands, then all round the drums, then back at us. 'Well I ain't out with *Darren 'Arvey*,' she goes.

Ol pulls on his bass, and nods to us.

'Just wanted to make you sweat a bit, Oliver,' says Gail. 'Time you learnt some *respect*. Now . . .'

BADABADABADABADA *SMASH*!

'... What's the first number?'

' 'Ang on, 'ang on,' says Ol. 'Ain't as simple as that, is it? C'mon, Wingnut, you ain't loud enough. You better play through me uvver amp. Bill ... no, you ain't in this one, are yer? Now just remember, Gail. We only just started practising. It ain't like drummin', yer know.'

'But what we playin'?' goes Wingnut.

'The number! The number!' goes Ol. 'A, G, F, E, right?'

'What's the song called?' goes Gail.

'Ready everyone?' goes Ol. 'One, two, free, *four!*'

I don't know what Ol was expecting. On one hand, you could say it was quite clever – the way no one was in tune, and *no one* was in time, and *everyone* managed to avoid playing *anything* that fitted in in *any* way with *anyone* else. On the other hand, you could say it was a bloody awful racket. Too much for me, any rate. After they'd all been blasting themselves silly for about two minutes, I decided to take a walk outside.

Peace! Tell you miss, never had the school playground looked so good. I say looked, but point of fact I couldn't see a thing. It was seven thirty and pitch black. Freezing and all. Still, a man's gotta do ...

I walk ten yards to the other corner of the annexe. I notice someone's stopped playing inside. I stop to listen. Hello, I thinks to meself – how come me footsteps are carrying on without me?

Miss, I am *not alone*!

'Whossat?' I go, trying to sound dead macho.

The footsteps come closer, along with someone's wheezy breath. I jump one way, then the other.

'S'all right,' says something, and I jump in the air and all.

'Yatesy!' I go. 'Whatcha doin' 'ere?'

Yatesy picks up a stone, and rolls it round in his hand. I'm ready for anything. He chucks it at the tennis court fence, and it comes bouncing back between us. I stare at it, like it's going to do a song and dance or something.

'You in that band, then?' says Yatesy.

'Why?' I go.

'Whatcha mean, why?'

'Whatcha mean, whatcha mean, why?'

Yatesy gives up. He brings back his foot and thwack! He kicks his pebble straight into me shin.

'Ow!'

'Soz! Wasn't aimin' at yer!'

Keeping me eye on him, I reach down and give me leg a good rub.

'You wanna come in or somethin'?' I ask him.

Yatesy shrugs.

'Cos it makes no odds to *me* if yer do,' I go.

Yatesy shrugs again, but when I make for the door, he's behind me.

Looks like the band's been making real progress since I went out. The bass guitar's on the floor, the drumsticks are back in Gail's bag, and Ol's hovering over Wingnut like a fly swatter. 'What you *doin'*, Wingnut?' he's going. 'I thought you was supposed to know about music!'

'It's you that ain't playin' in time, Oliver,' says Gail.

'Right,' says Ol, holding out his hand towards Gail. 'Giz them sticks. *You* play the bass if you know so much about it.'

KER-RASH! Wingnut's on the floor. He's pushed a table over, then gone and fallen on top of it. 'I'm leavin'!' he goes. 'We'll never do anything without a teacher!'

He's done it now. Ol's down in a flash, twisting Wingnut's arm up behind his back. 'You're *pafetic*, Wingnut! Soon as somefing's wrong, it's "Sir! Sir!" What you want – 'Atton in front of us, wavin' a stick?'

'Leave him alone, Oliver,' says Gail. 'Least teachers don't bully him like you do.'

Ol drops the arm, and turns on Gail again. It's then he notices me and Yatesy, stood by the door. That stops him quick enough.

'Er . . . all right if Yatesy watches us rehearse?' I go.

No, it wasn't all right. Nothing was all right. One practice, and we were ready to jack it in for good. Ol couldn't come to terms with the fact that our music wasn't going to be brilliant just cos he'd decided it would be. We had to work on it, and hard. We had to learn to play our instruments, but just as important, we had to learn to play *as a band*. And that wouldn't happen overnight.

Sad to say miss, it wouldn't happen to me at all. Soon as I got back from the practice, me old man read me the riot act. He reminded me, just in case I'd forgot, how he was the breadwinner, and provided a roof over me head, and never asked nothing in return but a bit of respect. And like I always do, I felt like saying I never *asked* to be born, except I knew he'd say he wished I wasn't.

Yes, there'd been a different attitude in me. I was starting to get as bad as the others at that school. I was *still* seeing Ol, despite what he said. I was *still* neglecting me homework, despite what he said. Worst of all, I was starting to *answer my father back*. What a shame it was, when I used to be such a model of good behaviour.

So. No more band.

'It ain't fair!' I says to him.

'*Life* ain't fair,' he says to me.

So what's new?

The band set up for their second practice like they were setting up for a funeral. I got the feeling no one seriously believed they'd ever play, or even get a song together. Ol never even bothered to tell me to pick up the guitar, and Wingnut set up in a corner, like he was rehearsing on his own. Then Gail moaned at Olly when he started reminding us about A, G, F and E, and we were all set for a repeat of the last shambles.

'Right,' says Ol. 'Today we'll do it different. Today *I'll* decide what we do, and you all listen to what I say. That way we'll get somefing *done*.'

I wait for Gail to jump down Ol's throat. She don't.

'All right, Oliver,' she says. 'D'yer wan me to play in 4/4 time or 6/8?'

'Just . . . foller the bass, that's all,' says Ol.

'What 'bout Wingnut then? You want him to play chords or a riff?'

Ol's mouth twitches.

'Well come on then, Oliver.'

' 'E can play what 'e likes! I don't give a toss!'

'No, that's the trouble. You only listen to yerself.'

'All right then, Mrs Big. What do *you* suggest?'

'I suggest . . . I set up a simple beat. Then you just practise fitting in with what I do. You can play them notes if you like, but *in time*. Then Wingnut's got some ideas he can do over the top.'

'How do you know?'

'We worked 'em out.'

'How?'

'Wiv 'elp from Mr Reaney, that's how.'

Click! Off goes Olly's amp.

Miss, sometimes I wonder how anything ever got done. How all them roads got laid, and hospitals got built, and football leagues got organized, and most of all how hit records got put together. It was a miracle, miss!

'Which is worse then, Oliver – us getting advice off someone who knows what they're talkin' about, or us being *told* what to do by someone who don't?'

'This is *our* band – not the *school choir*!'

'*Your* band, you mean!'

I was beginning to think me old man had done me a favour. Who needed it? Not Gail, any rate. She reached for her spanner and started loosening her drum. All right, says Ol, putting on a real sneery face, Let's Do What Teacher Says! So Gail puts down her spanner, and drums. Ol starts playing this real moron bass, plod-plod-plod-plod, and somewhere off in the distance, notes creep out of Wingnut's keyboard. But for all that, it is vaguely together. Till Ol quits, that is.

'What you stop for, Oliver?'

'This is *borin'*.'

'So? We gotta start somewhere, ain't we? Anyhow, it'd sound better if you was *tryin'* to make it sound good.'

' 'Ow can you make somefing that *easy* sound good?'

'Well, of course, you can't ... not less you're a *pro* bassist.'

That fixes Olly. Next time them drums start up, he ain't got no choice but to give it all he's got. With the other going harder, Wingnut gets up courage to turn up. And know what, miss? The band was playing music!

There's a cold draught up me back. It's that Yatesy again, creeping through the door. He sits down near me, and watches them, dead hard, like they're an orchestra or something. Ol notices him, and tries harder, and starts getting out of time. All of a sudden the music's a noise again. Ol stops, and glares at Wingnut, then has a go at Gail, then asks me where I was, and finally nods over at Yatesy and says What's E Want, Anyhow?

Everyone looks at Yatesy. He shrinks down. Then he jumps up and makes for the door.

'No, 'ang on,' says Gail.

Yatesy hangs on.

'You want to join in, don't yer?' says Gail.

Yatesy shrugs. Ol looks away, like he can't hear nothing.

'What's yer name?' says Gail.

'Martinyates,' burbles Yatesy.

'What yer do then, Martin?'

Yatesy shakes his head.

'He can sing,' I go.

Gail looks to Ol. Then Wingnut. Then me. 'Well,' she says. 'Seein' as we *do* wanna do this Christmas Show, and we *ain't* got a proper singer, I reckon we should give yer a try-out.'

Ol mumbles something, and Gail asks him if he's given up the idea of doing the show. She gets her way.

'Here y'are,' I says to Yatesy. 'You 'ave the mike.'

Suddenly, the air's tense. Old Yatesy grabs our mike with both hands, and stands there all rigid, like he's had an electric shock. He nods his head in time as the music starts up, and sets his worn-out eyes on the ceiling.

And then ... nothing.

'Just sing anythin'!' I say to him.

Yatesy hears me, but it makes no odds. His mouth opens, his fists tighten, he *strains* and *strains* to get into it, but still something holds him back.

'What's up?' Gail shouts over.

'I can't sing over this, can I?' says Yatesy, through the mike.

Suddenly, Ol goes crazy. 'Yeah!' he goes. 'Yeah! Do that!'

'What?' goes Yatesy.

'Rap!' goes Ol. 'Talk down the mike! That sounded *hard*, man!'

Yatesy ain't so sure. But he listens for the beat, gets himself set, and says the line again.

Ol's right!

Everyone knows something good's going to happen. The sound tightens up. Yatesy seizes on to the mike. He squeezes it till his hand shakes. Then, suddenly, there's words. Bucketfuls of words, spilling out of Yatesy's mouth, bouncing off the walls. At first, it's just nonsense. Then I start to pick out a few things. And I know them! I've heard them before! 'Come on Yatesy! Come on Yatesy! Come on Yatesy, what's an heir?' 'Get up on the table, get up and sing! Get up on the table or get done in!' I start to feel scared. It's vicious. It's lost control. It's like his whole system is just spewing up. You know, like he can't keep down all the crap that's in there. And then it's just nonsense again, like some old drunk babbling at you. But all the while he's smashing his spare hand against the mikestand, smash! smash! smash! enough to shatter every bone in his arm. Yet he don't seem to feel a thing.

Old Ol's like the cat that got the cream. You should've seen him, miss, grooving away with his great melon grin. He was the devil himself, Old Ol. For everything Yatesy shouted something back, or whooped, or screamed, or just dug into his bass till the room shook.

'I can't sing over this, can I?
I *can't* sing over this, can I?'

Third time round, and *everyone's* singing the chorus, including me. God knows what it sounded like outside, but mark my words, it was the best music *we'd* ever heard.

I can't tell you how long it went on for, I really can't. But I can tell you this – when it did stop, I was ready to *drop*. And I hadn't even been playing. *'Ye-eah!'* says Olly, giving his bass one last smack.

'Now, didn't I tell yer?' says Gail, smiling her head off.

I look round for Yatesy. He's sat on a chair, bent right over, staring at the floor. The only part of him that's moving is his knees, and that's because Olly's started pogoing round the room, shouting We're An Ace Band! We're An Ace Band! Wingnut joins in, and next thing he's being piggybacked round the room. Being Wingnut, he gets over-excited and headbutts the wall. Gail ties her scarf round his head, and Ol offers to give him a brain transplant.

The gear was light as a feather when we packed up that night. We tumbled out into the rain with Ol making raps on anything in sight, and ideas for new songs springing out of every little thing we said, or did, or even thought about. The big time was just around the corner. There was *nothing* this band couldn't do.

Winston picked Ol up after the practice, and they invited me down the Beeches with them – you know, that big adventure playground down Victoria Avenue.

'We gonna ask Yatesy?' I says.

'What for?' goes Ol.

' 'E's in the band now, ain't 'e?' I go.

No answer.

'Come on, Ol! Of course 'e is!'

Ol pokes the ground with his trainer. 'You ask 'im then,' he goes.

Yatesy didn't seem all together. He couldn't grab what I was on about when I told him we was going down the Beeches. Then when it did click, he took one look at Winston and shook his head.

'Tell yer what,' I says. 'If yer change yer mind, we'll be down there for a while yet. Winston's band practises there.'

Yatesy nods, makes with a flicker of a smile, and disappears. The others are on their buses by now, so it's just Ol and me that climbs up on Winston's front seat for one more version of the famous rap.

I'd always wondered about that house that stood next to the Beeches. I'd seen loads of people go in there, but I never seen none come out. Sort of swallowed them up, it did. When we was kids, people said it was a witches' house, and we used to run past it at ninety mile an hour, and imagine it chasing after us and sucking us down the chimney. But you know how it is with things that scare you when you're little. You just get to know more about them. Well, now that day had come.

Winston turned the key, and led us into this bare hallway, with faded-out flowery wallpaper and one dangling light bulb. There was rooms off both ways, but nothing in them except jumble. We pressed on down the end, then up these stairs. One floor, then another, then another. Ol fell over a kid's trike, then I fell over an electric drill, then both of us just missed a pile of broken glass. There was this smoky smell in the air, and it was getting stronger. I was starting to brick it. So, like yer do, I blabbed. 'Er . . . did I tell yer, Ol?'

'What?'

'Don't fink I did.'

'What?'

'I can't be in the band no more, Ol.'

'What?'

We stop. We're on the top landing, and there's nowhere to go. Winston props up a stepladder.

'Don't matter now, does it, Ol? Yatesy can sing. 'E can probably learn guitar an' all.'

'You been *told* to leave, ain't yer?'

'Ol, I can't do nuffink about it.'

'Lie. That's what I do.'

I shake me head. Winston calls Ol from the top of the ladder, just before he disappears through a hole in the ceiling. Ol jumps on after him, and climbs like a monkey. Well, who ain't been in an attic before? Just a few steps later, one big heave, and I'm there.

Now *hang on a second*!

Miss, I don't know where I'd come to, but it wasn't nowhere on *this* planet. Everything's lit up with this eerie red light, and there's fifteen, maybe twenty bodies looming up above me. All of them are black, and I swear they're ten foot tall. The room round them's *jammed* with gear – guitars, amps, drums, and *massive* speakers. All over the walls is this dark woolly stuff, like the attic's wearing a jumper. There's posters, and flags, and talk, and music, and thick smelly smoke everywhere. And there's Olly, in the middle of it all, sat up on a speaker like some kind of mascot. I reach out and tug the bottom of his jeans. 'Where are we?' I go.

'Leggo mi leg, ya *ras-claat*.'

'Eh?'

'I-an-I is gwan back to wi *roots*.'

'Do what? Speak English, will yer?'

I suddenly get one of them moments when you ain't sure of nothing. *Is* it Ol? Which one's Winston? Are they *all* Winston? Can anyone *see* me?

Yes, it's Ol alright. He's started rattling on about the group, and how big we are, and how hard his bass playing is. He's right at home, is Ol. Maybe this was what he was after. Him and his own group, in a world of their own, with their mates dropping in to listen and no idea even of what time it was. Somewhere where *school* looked stupid, not you. I mean, imagine Hatton up in that attic, telling Ol to do his button up!

Hello. They're talking about me. Someone's asking if I'm in the band, and Ol's saying yes.

'No!' I go, and me voice comes out like the weediest note on a school recorder.

' 'E's the roadie,' says Ol, covering himself.

'Waa-aa-haa!'

The whole room's swallowed up with laughing. Great rolling tides of it, shaking everyone's chests and drowning out the sound system. I pop back down like a rabbit, and make for home. The stairs collapse around me and the bannisters are on fire. Well, not really, but they might as well have been.

Ol catches me in the bottom hallway.

' 'Ang on, Bill! Don't yer wanna be the roadie? Where yer goin'?'

' 'Ome!' I throw open the front door, then stop in me tracks. Yatesy's at the front gate.

'All right?' he goes, dead nervous.

Ol edges up by me. He comes over kind of serious, and nods at Yatesy.

'What yer doin' then?' goes Yatesy.

'Not much,' goes Ol.

'Oh yeah?' says Yatesy.

'Wanna come in then?' says Ol.

'Anyone else around?' says Yatesy.

'Not in the yard,' goes Ol.

'All right then,' goes Yatesy.

We walk back down the hallway, but this time instead of going up the stairs Ol draws the bolt on the back door. And what do you know? It's the door to the playground. Quite light it is, with the moon out, but empty as the North Pole. Without saying nothing, Ol makes straight for the ski lift. That's that big scaffolding affair you can see above the wall outside. You got to climb up one end, grab hold of a pulley-wheel, then push off down the ropes and into the sand-pit at the other end. I hate it. It's like one of them bad dreams, flying down hill in a car with no brakes.

We get to the top.

'Goin' on?' says Ol to Yatesy.

Yatesy don't hang around. He grabs hold of the pulley next to Ol's, yanks it back, and whoof! They're off. They rattle down the ropes till they're just rag dolls in the distance, plonking into the sand.

The big slide's next. Ol goes flat on his back, so Yatesy goes down like a bullet, on his front. I just go down.

Yatesy runs for the tyre wall, and we follow. Then it's the witch's hat, the tunnels, and the tree-ropes. We don't miss out on one little thing. No one to get at us, no one to tell us what to do – it was just too good to be true. By the time we hit the swings, I'm that knackered I could sleep for a week. But we don't stop there.

'First one over the top!'

Off we go, kicking out and bucking the swings till me stomach turns over something rotten. Wooh! That's enough for me. Not Ol and Yatesy though. Them two, they just go higher and higher and higher, till what was high looks low, and what was impossible looks easy. Suddenly I start to wonder if Ol's joking or not. They ain't stopping! The idiots are racing each other over the top!

I can't look!

'All right! All right – joke! Joke, Yatesy!'

I look. God, they must have been near on level with the top bar. But the kicking and stretching's stopped now, and slowly they're coming down. After a bit, everything's relaxed. We're all swinging along in a line, nice and gentle like. And we've put out that much heat, the whole night's come up warmer.

' 'Ere, Yatesy,' says Ol.

'What?'

' 'Ow come you got kicked out your last school, then?'

'Fightin'.'

'Who d'yer fight wiv?'

'Ev'ryone.'

'Ev'ryone?'

'Black kids, mainly.'

'Whysat, then? You prejudiced?'

'Dunno. Don't think so.'

'Well how come, then?'

Yatesy scuffs at the ground with his toe. 'S'pose it started when me dad lost 'is job,' he goes. 'I never understood it, cos his firm said it was cos of computers, but then this kid comes up to me at school an' says 'is dad's got my dad's old job. My dad was a troublemaker, he said.'

'That's what they call me,' says Ol.

'Well anyhow, this kid keeps taking the piss out of me, and showing me his new bike, and his cassette, and his watch. And meanwhile my old man's just losin' 'ope, you know? One day I just couldn't take it no more. I smacked him in. He knew he couldn't get me back, so he started up all these rumours instead. They was just *lies*. He said I hated black kids, and picked on 'em. Next thing, they're comin' lookin' for me. Then all the teachers notice I keep getting in scraps with black kids, so in the end, *everyone* believes it. I was fighting every day, by the time they kicked me out.'

'What 'bout Canning, then?'

'Oh yeah. Same thin' again. Once you get a *reputation* . . .'

'Yeah. I know.'

'This school, me old man's told me to keep meself to meself, an' really *try* to work. But 'e don't really believe it'll 'appen. 'E don't really believe nuffin'll 'appen no more.'

'Yeah. My mum's like that. She thought England was goin' to be *so* great, y'know? Now she just does piece-work at 'ome, for *piss-all*, an' talks about goin' back to Jamaica to die.'

All of a sudden, Ol's eyes flash up and fix on Yatesy's. 'Ain't *my* fault, is it?' he goes.

'No,' says Yatesy.

Somehow I know I should just push off. So I do. As I reach the door out, I hear Ol say This Band's Gonna Be Brilliant, Ain't It Yatesy?

'Dunno,' says Yatesy. 'Try, I s'pose.'

'We'll show 'em.'

I don't know who Ol was on about, and I don't reckon Ol did neither. But maybe it didn't matter.

5

If my old man ever found out I lied to him, I'd be looking for a new family. I told him I was joining Basketball Club on Fridays after school. That way I'd miss the Monday and Wednesday rehearsals, but I'd be able to help out on Fridays shifting gear and that. I've always been told lying's the worst sin you can do, unless you're filling in a tax return or using yesterday's car park ticket. But I couldn't say I felt bad about it – just scared.

Yatesy give Ol a nice friendly smile next time they saw each other at school. Ol's mouth did a kind of lightning twitch, then he was off somewhere else on urgent business. Yatesy never seemed too surprised about it. Still, the next two rehearsals went good, according to Ol. Seeing as Yatesy said he'd got a bad throat, they decided to work on just music. They wrote this new song called Answering Machine, which come about from Wingnut saying 'What d'you want me to do?' all the time. Ol'd learnt C, D and F sharp, so he did something on them notes, and Gail set up a good beat to go with them. Things were working together that much quicker now the band could see something coming of it.

Meanwhile, Yatesy'd been picking up Reaney's guitar and mucking about with it. Ol said that if Yatesy played his cards right, Ol'd teach him everything he knew. With a bit of hindrance off Reaney, of course. Yatesy said all right, he was keen.

He had to be. The Christmas Show was six weeks off, and already the Art department was getting the info for the programmes. Some fifth year come up our tutor room and asked Ol and me what the band's name was.

'Wingnut an' the Bolts,' I says.

'Ang on, 'ang on, no it ain't,' says Ol, and tells the fifth year to come back in ten minutes, while he remembers what the real name is. He says to me that Wingnut and the Bolts was just a joke name. For a reggae band, you got to have something *rootsy*.

'It ain't a reggae band, is it?' I go.

'Course it is!' says Ol. 'Now, what 'bout callin' it after a song? Somefin' like . . . *Soul Rebels* . . . or *Trench Town Rockers*.'

'Why don't yer just call it Oliver's Army?' I go, feeling really sarcy.

'Yeah!' goes Ol. 'That's a *sound* idea – Oliver's Army!'

'It's a joke, Ol!'

'Bill, 'ave I ever told you you're a genius? 'Ere, where's that fifth year?'

We'd got a problem. It was the second Friday I'd seen

them rehearse, and we still couldn't get a word out of Yatesy. The band had got the backing really tight now, and even worked out a couple of stops and a rhythm change. But what was the use, if he wouldn't get up there and rap?

'Let's forget it,' says Ol, switching off.

' 'Ang about, Oliver,' says Gail. 'Listen, Yatesy – don't yer *wanna* sing, or what?'

Yatesy can't say.

'Well – is it that you don't like the song . . . or the way we're doin' it . . . or what?'

Yatesy still can't say.

'Let's put it this way,' says Ol. 'We rehearse it now, or we drop it.'

'That ain't gonna encourage him, is it Oliver?' says Gail. 'You just put people off when you press 'em like that.'

That's enough for Ol. He takes a deep breath, stomps across the room, and grabs the mike off Yatesy.

'Listen,' he says. 'This band's goin' on stage in a few weeks, right? On *stage*, right, in front of a *audience*, right? If Yatesy can't do it now in front o' four people, what's 'e gonna be like in front o' four 'undred? Eh?'

'You still ain't 'elpin', Ol,' says Gail.

'Give me strength!' goes Ol, kicking the nearest chair.

'Look,' says Gail. 'Let's give it a break. You still ain't listened to Wingnut's new tune yet.'

'No!' goes Ol. 'I won't give it a break! I know what I'm talkin' about, right? When you get up on stage you got to know what you're doin'. You either *perform*, or you *die*. An' we're gonna *perform*. 'Ere – do the music again.'

Gail and Wingnut look at each other, sort of weary, then start up the backing to Yatesy's rap.

'Right, Yatesy,' says Ol. 'You're a good singer, right? But you got to *pose about a bit*.'

Ol sets off round the room with the mike, like some kind of demented pigeon. He starts rapping a load of nonsense, the kind of thing he does in Drama and everyone laughs at. Now and then his legs give way, and he drops on his knees. Then up he jumps again, swinging the mike on its lead, twisting his hips, and shaking his fist on the choruses.

When he's done, Gail suggests again they listen to Wingnut's tune.

'All right then,' says Ol. 'I'll sing.'

'You're set on that, are yer?' says Gail.

'Yeah.'

'Right.'

Gail jumps off her stool and heads for Olly's gear.

'What yer doin'?' says Ol.

'Playin' bass!'

Ol's stumped. 'You can't do that,' he says. 'Who's gonna play drums?'

'Come on, Wingnut,' says Gail.

Half a minute later, and the new band's complete. Wingnut's got the sticks, and I'm behind the keyboard. Ol looks round at us lot, shakes his head, and then starts to laugh.

'OK, band,' he goes. 'We're on stage, right? The curtain's goin' up, an' 'alf the school's out there waiting for us. I'm gonna count to four, an' then we're gonna *'it 'em wiv it*, right? One . . . two . . . free . . . *four!*'

Well, we 'it 'em with it, all right.

'There,' says Ol, when the whole din's come clattering to a halt. 'What was wrong wi' that, then?'

'This band'll never get nowhere till yer do what I say!' says Gail, smacking the bass guitar.

'We need a teacher!' I go, putting on this sulky little face.

'Shut up about teachers, Wingnut!' goes Gail to me.

'Don't you wanna do the rap, Yatesy?' says Wingnut to Ol.

Ol sinks into this pathetic heap. But he can't stop a grin sneaking out. Yatesy watches him, sort of interested.

'Anyway,' says Gail. 'What's this new tune, Wingnut?' She walks over and stands ten inches off me nose. 'Come on! Let's 'ear it! What's keepin' yer?'

That sets them all off. I crouch there behind me keyboards as Gail, Wingnut and Olly bear down on me, clapping their hands and going 'Wing*nut*! Wing*nut*! Wing*nut*!' Louder and louder they get, and closer and closer till I can't hardly breathe. 'Wing*nut*! Wing*nut*! Wing*nut*!'

Miss Harris, I *was* Wingnut. I had jug-ears and boss-eyes and snobby parents. God, they had it in for me, that lot.

Get me out of this!

'Wing*nut*! Wing*nut*! Wing*nut*!'

'Quit it!'

Ol falls over laughing, Gail and all. But shutting up Wingnut was another matter.

The order of the Christmas Show was announced at the start of December. The band got a ten minute slot right after the interval, just before the choir. Ol was furious we never got more time, and went to see Disco about it, seeing as he ran the thing. Disco told us it was his job to please the Head, and it was the Head's job to please the governors, the politicians, local industry, the papers, and the parents – people like our mums and dads. Well who's school run for, says Ol, if it ain't kids that go there?' That's a very amusing thought, says Disco.

Ol was getting to be an embarrassing person to hang round with. Whenever someone asked him about the band, he made all these stupid claims, like we was going to blow the rest of the Christmas Show off the stage, or have a party after the gig with twenty-five groupies, or turn pro within the next two years. It was like all the controls had gone between his brain and his mouth. But when it come down to talking about who else was in this band, he just disowned the lot of them. If Gail and Wingnut was playing, that was cos they was last minute replacements who'd get ditched straight after the gig.

Yatesy never got mentioned, never. Ol went on about 'Answering Machine' and this other song he wrote called 'Close the Door, It's Freezing Out', but never about Yatesy's rap. I'd heard all the songs, and I could see they were getting more *musical*, but to be honest, I could take 'em or leave 'em, you know? Nothing had ever been a patch on Yatesy, that second rehearsal. But could we get him to do it again? Not a hope. All he'd do was work on his guitar chords, and it had got to the point where no one bothered to ask no more.

Ol made a poster. He showed it me.

'I'm gettin' two hundred done,' he goes.

'*Two hundred*? Where you gonna put 'em?'

'All round town. Cover up all the uvver bands' posters.'

'But no one's gonna come from town to see the *school show*, are they, Ol?'

Ol whips the poster away from me. 'You're givin' me negative vibes, man,' he says.

Miss, why does it matter? Why've we *got* to know when tadpoles grow back legs, when all we want to work on is our music? The more the term went on, the more the homework piled up. Even Wingnut got behind. He must've left the band thirty times. 'But what about the Science?' he'd go. 'Do it in Drama,' Ol'd go. 'But what about the English?' 'Do it in Drama'.

You see miss, Reaney trusted people. If they'd got something wrong with their feet, they could not use the drama studio, and that was that. Mind you, even Reaney must've had his doubts about the plague of verrucas, whitlows and athlete's foot that come over our band every Friday afternoon.

A week or so before the show, Reaney said we was doing these 'mirror exercises'. That's where one person's got to do something, or say something, and the rest've got to follow it, close as they can. Ickie volunteers first, and gets them all peeling oranges, running on the spot, and tying themselves in knots trying to copy his yoga positions. Then Ick starts going stupid, and picking his nose and things, so Reaney's got to stop it before the lesson gets out of hand. 'Thank you very much,' he says. 'From now on, *I* shall be the leader.'

'Thank you very much,' says Ickie. 'From now on *I* shall be the leader.'

'Don't be silly now,' says Reaney.

'Don't be silly now,' says half a dozen others.

Ol puts down his homework.

'OK,' says Reaney, waving his arms about. 'Good joke. That'll do now.'

'OK,' says everyone else in the room, waving their arms about. 'Good joke. That'll do now.'

Reaney marches across the room, flings open the door, and tells us to all line up outside again. Except everyone's right there behind him, telling *him* to line up outside again. He slams the door, and it slams and slams again, twenty-three times. We copy anything and everything he does, except the big purple vein coming up on his forehead.

At last Ol can't stay out no more. He jumps into the middle of the floor and says he's taking over as leader. Before Reaney can breathe again, Ol's led the whole class across the studio, up the ladder, and on to the catwalk. We start singing, like the seven dwarfs, and end up marching on the spot, like soldiers, against the far wall.

Ol changes the rules slightly. Now, instead of us just copying him, he's giving orders. 'Come on, you useless shower!' says Ol. 'Get them heads up!'

Great laugh, it is. Ol parades down the line, fixing a button here, a bent arm there. Reaney makes one last-ditch attempt to save the lesson by pretending to be a senior officer, but Ol denounces him as an imposter, and has Azi and Kev put him in the dungeon behind the piano. 'Belly in!' says Ol to Fat Brian. 'Oh, sorry – it *is* in, is it?

'To the left – quick march!' says Ol, and the whole class tramp over to the side wall. 'Did I say halt?' says Ol. 'Up the wall, you layabouts!'

Ickie laughs, and Ol whacks him one with a stick he's picked up. 'I mean it!' he goes.

Ickie stands there, kind of hurt and shocked. Ol prods him into the wall.

'Careful, Ol,' says Angie.

'How dare you talk back to an officer!' Ol screams into her face.

'Come on, Ol,' says someone else.

'Who said that?'

Ol pushes another girl back against the wall, and starts ranting on at her like a maniac. She starts crying. Other girls come round and back her up. Ol gets worse. Some of the boys start calling themselves Ol's strike force, and pick on the girls. In half a minute, we've got chaos. The girls are all down one end, half of them in tears and the rest of them screaming at Olly, and the boys are down the other, shouting out insults and calling them all slags and creeps. Reaney sits behind the piano, with his head in his hands. He's given up.

Then Hatton walks in.

'What the *hell* is going on? Where's your teacher?'

Silence. Reaney don't move, apart from his eyes.

'Am I talking a foreign language? I *said*, where is your teacher?'

Reaney's still frozen. One by one, everyone's eyes have turned to him. Hatton paces forwards, with his head craning round.

He's seen him.

'Oh,' says Hatton.

Reaney creeps out of his hidey-hole. 'Er . . .,' he says.

'I'm sorry, Mr Reaney,' says Hatton. 'I'll leave you to get on with your lesson.'

Hatton scours the room one last time, and keeps his eyes on Ol. Then he marches out. But his shadow hangs on, watching over Reaney's lesson and these wimpy little plays we do about discovering new planets. Reaney sits out, looking grim. Ol's the slimiest boot-licker you ever seen, talking in this soft little voice, and looking round every ten seconds to check if Reaney's watching him. At the end of the lesson, while the rest are putting on their shoes, Ol puts on a sick little smile and asks Reaney if it might be all right to borrow some of the school play cossies for wearing on stage.

Reaney asks Ol if he's joking. Ol says he never jokes, not ever.

'Well the answer's no,' says Reaney. 'Most certainly not.'

Ol's face drops. 'Go on, sir!' he goes. 'Sorry 'bout the lesson,' he goes.

Reaney's head jerks up, so sudden it makes us jump. 'No you're not!' he goes. 'You're not sorry one bit! You don't give a *damn* about ruining this lesson, or the one before that, or the one before that! I'm a soft touch, aren't I? Good for a joke! Do you think I don't notice how you take advantage of me? It doesn't matter what I do for you, what I lend you, how much time I spend on you and your *group* – you'll still come back the next day and walk all over me, won't you?'

Ol smiles, a nervous smile.

'Going to be a rasta, like your brother, are you?' says Reaney. 'This is brotherhood, is it? This is justice for all, is it?'

Reaney's eyes boil at Olly. Ol's face has turned to stone. He picks up his shoes and walks out, in his socks.

Reaney lets out a deep breath.

'Maybe you should be stricter with us,' I go.

Reaney looks at me, biting his lip, like there's something he's got to explain to me. I leave.

Ol kept his stoneface right through last period, and it

was still there on him when he walked into rehearsal. No one said a thing as we set up, and I'd seen more energy in a graveyard.

'Let's do my new one then,' says Ol, still sat on his chair.

There's a quick glance between Gail and Wingnut.

'We ain't really that keen on it,' says Gail.

'Oh,' says Ol.

'It's a bit like the uvver two, ain't it?' says Gail.

'Dunno,' says Ol.

'Well,' says Gail. 'Shall we run through "Answering Machine", then?'

Ol shrugs, and stubs at the notes. He stays sat down when the song starts, and the whole thing limps along, half out of time, and sounds *awful*. Yatesy plays the latest chords he's learned with no mistakes, but when he sings Ol's words, it's like he's singing Russian or something.

> 'You're like an answering machine
> You always says the same thing
> You're like an answering machine
> And you're going in the bin.'

And I thought playing music was for fun.

'Great,' says Gail, when they've done. 'If we play like that next Friday, we're gonna get bottled off stage.'

'You got two more practices yet,' I go, trying to cheer things up a bit.

'When's the next practice, then?' says Ol.

'You what?' I go. 'You know when it is – next Monday!'

'Oh,' says Ol. 'Can't make it then.'

'What you talking about?' says Gail.

'Already arranged somefing,' says Ol.

Gail can't believe it. 'Oliver, it's the second-to-last practice! These songs still ain't ready!' she says.

'Look, I don't let down me mates, right?' says Ol.

Gail puts down her sticks. 'What yer mean, Oliver?' she says.

'What I said,' says Ol. 'I told Dan I'll go out wiv 'im, I'll *go* out wiv 'im.'

The rest of us look from one to another. You can read it on every face, what they're thinking. Except Yatesy. He ain't nothing but a blank, blank page.

For ten years I'd been bringing back letters from school, all neatly folded, put in evelopes, and addressed to me mum and dad. And for ten years, me old man'd been opening them, going Hm! and dropping them in the bin. So when I took back the letter about the Christmas Show, I never thought no more of it. Then out of the blue, me old man forks out two quid and asks me to get him a couple of tickets. As he does it, he watches my face.

I went to see Reaney at the weekend. I'd been thinking how I'd set the gear up for the band, and I realized I never knew nothing about playing in big halls. When you see these concerts on telly, they've got these massive speaker systems on both sides of the stage, and I think there's a bloke working the controls somewhere and all. Our gear wasn't quite up to that.

No one answered Reaney's door, but it was open. I crept up the stairs into the hall, and for a moment, I thought I'd wandered in the wrong house. Dead tidy, it was. Then I noticed a dinner plate with a pile of books on it and I knew I'd got the right place.

I found Reaney in the bedroom. He was bent over his desk, writing, with cups of coffee all round him. 'All right, sir?' I go.

Reaney flies backwards like he's touched the mains. Clouds of papers go scattering round the room, cups and saucers with them. Reaney winds up sprawled over the floor, scrabbling at the bedspread and gasping for air.

'All right if I come in?' I go.

Reaney struggles back onto his chair, holding his heart. 'Please . . . do remember to knock,' he goes.

'Sorry sir. What you workin' on, sir?'

I lean over Reaney's shoulder and look at what he's writing.

'2r's Yatesy's class, ain't it sir?' I go.

'That's right.'

> **Lesson**
> 2r, Period 4, 14th December
>
> **Aims**
> To foster group trust and physical co-ordination in a dramatic milieu.
>
> **Materials**
> 14 blindfolds, various tactile objects.
>
> **Procedure**
> Class split into groups of 6 and 7 and form circles. One member of the

'You better be strict on them, sir. They're trouble, sir.'

Reaney picks up the paper and frowns at it.

'Bill . . .,' he says.

'Yeah?'

'Do you think I'll ever make a teacher?'

What do you say?

'The thing is,' says Reaney, 'this is my third term of teaching. At the end of a year, there's a kind of *report* . . . which says if you've passed or failed.'

'I 'spect you'll pass,' I go.

Reaney looks up to me, all hopeful. 'Do you really think so?' he says.

'Oh yeah,' I go, like a world expert.

Reaney thinks about it, and I start tidying up some of these papers I've sent all over the room.

'I've got an inspector coming,' says Reaney. 'This lesson with 2r next Friday, you see. And if he doesn't like what he sees . . .'

I open Reaney's little bedside drawer to put some papers away. There's a sandwich in there.

'The thing is, Bill,' says Reaney, 'this school's got to lose some teachers. The money's been cut back. And I'm not the most popular person in high places.'

I poke the sandwich to check it ain't alive.

'Why don't they like yer then, sir?' I go.

'Several reasons. And one of them's the way I've got involved with you lot.'

'Why, sir? You're helpin' us.'

'Perhaps. But it is regarded as *unprofessional*. Using the cane is thought of as *professional*, but me helping you lot is *unprofessional*. That's the way things are, at the moment.'

'Oh. I see.'

I didn't.

'No point in me askin' yer about the show then, I suppose,' I go.

'What do you need?' says Reaney.

The moment I opened that door I knew something was wrong. Gail and Wingnut were sat on their cases, looking serious. None of the gear was set up.

Ol come in behind me, still swaggering from his Monday night out. 'What's up wiv you lot?' he goes.

'It's *Wednesday night*,' he goes. '*Last practice*. Two soddin' 'ours to get everythin' right!'

Gail flicks a toffee paper off her drum stool. It skids across the floor, and leaves a little trail in the dust. She looks up at Ol, eyes dead steady.

'Yatesy's quit the band,' she says.

Ol laughs. 'No 'e ain't!' he goes.

Gail holds out a hand, towards the mike stand and Yatesy's empty chair.

'Where is 'e, anyhow?' says Ol.

'He's *quit the band*, Oliver! He come in ten minutes ago, told us he was sorry, picked up his words and walked out.'

'Ha!'

'What's 'e quit for then?' says Ol.

'Well I don't fink it was nothing to do wiv *us*, Oliver.'

'What d'yer mean? What've *I* done?'

Gail buttons up. Ol starts to prowl the room. He barges into a table, and kicks the wall. Then he lashes out at Yatesy's chair, and sends it clattering into the mike stand and the whole lot crashing to the floor. 'All that work!' he goes. 'All that work, an' 'e chickens out now! I *knew* he ain't got no guts! That stupid . . . prejudiced . . . chicken . . . scaley-face! He set out to shit us up from the start! An' you lot . . . you just got took in, didn't yer?'

Ol belts Yatesy's chair again, and it just misses me. He turns on the others like they're something he wouldn't step in. 'Always *me* that's wrong, ain't it?' he says, thumping his chest. Gail starts to breathe deep.

'You *knew* what you were doin'.' she says. 'You knew what it meant, you standin' us up for them *pigs*.'

Ol grabs for Gail's sleeve. Gail whips her arm away, with her eyes in flames.

'Don't you touch me!' she goes.

'Well don't call my mates pigs!'

'Well they *are* pigs. Just cos they got big muscles, just cos they gang up together, they think they rule this school. They don't rule *no one*, no more than Hatton rules you, or you rule *us*.'

'I never said I ruled you.'

Gail reaches into her jacket and pulls out a programme for the Christmas Show. She holds it up to Olly, right up to his face.

'We're just the army, remember?' she says. 'We never make no decisions. Not even about the *name*.'

Ol snatches the programme, reads it, and smiles. 'Looks good, dunnit?' he says.

Wingnut punches his case.

'*I* don't care what it's called,' he goes. 'We're not even *in* the group after this concert. You ask anyone.'

'Who asked your opinion, Wingnut?' says Ol, sneering.

'Not you, that's for sure,' says Wingnut.

Ol keeps his eyes on Wingnut, trying to think up something funny, but Wingnut don't look away. Ol simmers. Then he boils. 'Who gives a *shit* about this *pissy* group, anyhow?' he goes. 'You fink I need it? You fink I need you? You must be jokin'! I could've been out havin' a good time this term, stead of gettin' cooped up 'ere wiv a *girl*, an' a *creep*, an . . .' Ol looks at me, '. . . a *daddy's boy*.'

Gail picks up her bass drum case and humps it towards the door. Then Wingnut rolls up his keyboard lead. Ol watches, arms folded, as bit by bit they pack their gear and take it to the door.

'C'mon, Wingers,' says Gail. 'I'll go an' ring me mum.'

'Don't worry,' says Ol. 'I don't need yer. I'll get 'old of a drum machine, an' make some backin' tapes. I can do everythin' meself, an' the singin' an' all.'

'Good,' says Gail. 'Then you won't 'ave no one else to blame for what comes out, will yer?'

Ol smiles, a big, false smile, until all he's smiling at is an empty room. Then he drops into a chair and stares at Gail's toffee paper. 'Drum machine,' he says, half to himself. 'Know anyone wiv one, do yer?'

'I ain't a daddy's boy,' I go.

'P'raps we could *make* a drum machine,' says Ol.

I find myself walking out. I just catch one glimpse of Ol as the door closes, looking up, as lost and helpless as a little baby. There's no sign of Gail and Wingnut outside, and I just wait there a while, feeling sick to the roots. Hopeless.

But wait. There's voices. Voices, and tramping steps. Gail and Wingnut appear round the corner of the tennis courts, nod at me, and march back into the hut. Gail goes straight over to her cases, and starts unbuckling one of them. Wingnut helps with another. Ol notices what's happening, but tries not to show nothing.

'You might give us some help,' says Gail to Olly.

Ol leaves it a few seconds, then shambles over to pull out a drum. He keeps his eyes well away from Gail's, but Gail watches him, watches his every move, like a hawk. 'This is our band, Oliver,' she says, at last. 'Our band, not just yours. An' we ain't givin' up now, just because you're too pig ignorant to see that.'

Ol don't argue. And that, Miss Harris, was a major breakthrough.

6

It seemed as if the whole world had left it to the last possible second to save their skins. The school stank of glue and paint and from bodged-up props for the staff panto. First years wandered through the cloakrooms reciting poems to themselves with desperate little faces. And from every other room you could hear dance steps counted, recorders turned up, and paper snowflakes snipped out.

Meanwhile, we sat it out. It may have been the day of the show, but as far as Hatton was concerned, it was Still A Normal School Day. So he droned on as usual through *Nowhere To Run* by Ursula Masters, while I watched a couple of fifth years through the windows, laying out cones for the VIP cars. Next to me, Ol scribbled messages, messages cancelling the first messages, and messages asking if I'd passed on the second message.

Eventually some idiot passes one message on to Hatton. Hatton immediately tells Ol to take up the reading. Ol scrabbles at his book.

'You are on the right page, I assume?' says Hatton.

'Yes, sir. Ninety-three, sir.'

'Oh really?'

Ol takes a quick shuftie at my book. He needn't have bothered. I'm on eighty-five.

Soon as the dinner bell goes, we get straight down the hall. Reaney's up on stage, in between two *murderous* great stacks of speakers. Our sound system for tonight.

'Wah, thanks, sir!' I shout up.

Reaney smiles at me, swaps a cagey glance with Ol, and starts reeling out a thick grey cable down the hall. We join him at the back, where there's a control panel to beat Concorde's.

'That's the mixer,' I tell Ol.

'Oh.'

'Bill and I will be working this tonight,' says Reaney.

I stand up behind it, and twist a couple of knobs. Gonna be some jealous people out there in the audience tonight.

'Right, Bill,' says Reaney. 'Get on stage and try out the mikes, will you? Bill? Are you all right?'

'Oh . . . yeah.'

Ol and me run back down the front, vault the stage, and spend the next ten minutes talking nonsense over the p.a., while odd bunches of kids wander in and watch. The sound comes up soft, then loud, then boomy, then hissy, till Reaney's happy he's got it right. Then I spend another ten minutes at the mixer, learning which instruments are coming through which channels, and how to make them more echoey, and where the on-switches are. I can't help but notice Reaney's hands are shaking on the controls. 'You ain't nervous about tonight an' all, are yer sir?' I go.

'I'm nervous about this afternoon,' says Reaney.

'Oh yeah. Your inspector, ain't it?'

'Mm.'

'Give 'em 'ell, sir!' I tell him. 'You can do it!'

'I'll certainly try,' says Reaney.

The afternoon's just one whole mess of last minute plans, then changes of plan, then back to how we had it in the first place. The band finally agrees to do 'Answering Machine' and 'Close The Door', with Olly singing. Seeing as Ol can't sing and play at the same time too good, Wingnut's going to have to do bits of the bass on his keyboards, besides his chords, and riffs, and solos. For once, Ol spends a whole half day without putting down Wingers. He's just great, Wingers.

And then we're there, sitting on the edge of the stage, with the gear in the wings, the clock ticking towards five, and rows and rows of empty seats in front of us. Gail and Wingnut are off somewhere looking for a chippy, and no one's got a clue where Reaney is. Sometime before the show, we're supposed to do a sound check. With the number of bodies milling round behind us I'm starting to doubt we'll get the chance. 'Maybe we should 'ave a word wiv Disco,' I go.

'What's the point?' says Ol. ' 'E won't understand.'

I pull out a packet of Rolos.

'No fanks,' says Ol. 'Not 'ungry.'

'Neither am I.'

Ol bends down and picks up a programme. He reads it over for the tenth time.

Yeah, we're still on.

'Your mum comin'?' I go.

'Yeah. They saved a few seats for 'er.'

We both laugh.

'My old man's comin' too,' I go.

' 'E ain't, is 'e? 'E *never* comes down 'ere.'

'I know. An' when 'e sees me, 'e's gonna know I lied to 'im. 'E'll kill me.'

'Save yer catchin' up wiv yer 'omework,' says Ol.

A bunch of first years turn up and start putting numbers on the chairs. Old Armitage is directing them, dressed as a fairy godmother.

'Just think, Ol,' I go. ' 'Alf an 'our an' every one o' them seats is goin' to 'ave someone sat on it – watchin' *our* band! Ain't they, Ol?'

'Which way's the bog?' says Ol.

Twenty to five. We're hiding from the rain in the bike sheds, and trying to get our breath back. We've been just about everywhere searching for Gail, and Wingnut, and

Reaney. Now it's dark. A big grey Merc draws up near us, and out gets this couple, not that old. The bloke sniffs around him, then takes the woman's arm. Just as they're going into school, she shakes him off again.

'Who's 'e?' I go.

''E's one o' the guests, ain't 'e?' says Ol. Ol slouches out and round the car. 'Look at that!' he goes. 'Quadrophonic speakers!'

'Wonder what sort o' music they like?' I go.

Ol kicks a tyre. 'Yunno somefin'?' he says. 'I 'ope 'e don't like us. I 'ope 'e really *'ates* us.'

'Still,' I go. 'We'll all 'ave one o' these, won't we? After the first 'it.'

'Nah,' says Ol. 'I been thinkin' about it. I reckon we should get a bloody great *artic*. The band can all get in the front, then the gear, an' we'll 'ave a gym in the back. Then we just roll into town, see, wiv our name on the side, an' we'll be just like the circus comin' into town, an' we'll start a *revolution*.'

'Yeah,' I go. 'Don't fancy the gym much, though.'

'You wouldn't.'

'Eh – remember when you an' Yatesy nearly went over the top bar?'

Ol's head drops. 'Shit,' he goes.

'What's up?'

''E should be playin' tonight.'

'Ain't the same, is it?'

Ol's mind starts to drift. Till he catches sight of his watch, that is. 'Hell!' he goes. 'Look at the time! We're s'posed to be doin' a sound check!'

We never got our sound check, Miss Harris. By the time we got back to the hall, people were already filing into their seats, and Gail and Wingnut were stood backstage, looking grey. 'Where've *you* been?' says Gail.

'Where've *you* been?' says Ol.

'Where's Mr Reaney?' says Wingnut.

Ol looks about. 'Yeah – where *is* 'e?' he goes.

'Come on, you lot! Out of my way!' McAdam barges past us, dressed as Cinderella, with a gym ramp. His little army follows him, carrying the rest of the gear for their display. We squeeze into a corner and crouch down, feeling dead young, and small, and useless. On the other side of the curtain, the footsteps have turned into a rumble. It's filling up fast.

'Everyone remembers that new bit in "Machine", don't they?' says Ol.

Wingnut's frozen.

'Wingnut!' goes Ol. 'You remember it, don't yer?'

'Where's Mr Reaney?' squeaks Wingnut.

'You're all right,' says Gail, patting Wingnut on the back. ''Ere, 'old 'is 'and, will yer Ol?'

Ol looks at Wingnut's pudgy white paw, and swallows. 'Listen, Wingnut,' he goes. ''Ave I ever told you you're a brilliant musician? Cos you are. An' we're all gonna play the most best we ever done tonight. Seen?'

Wingnut manages a smile. But there's not a lot left of it when that curtain goes up.

'God! Look at 'em all!'

Now we *all* freeze. We stare out over the stage into a wall of light, and behind it a whole race of coughing, rustling, waiting bodies. The first pair of feet patter over to the gym horse. There's a thump, and a crack of applause, then a bigger thump, and a roar of laughter. McAdam comes past us carrying a first year, who's in agony.

Disco told us the first half of the show'd last thirty odd minutes. But believe me, it went on hours, and hours, and *hours*. And as for that poet who was last on before us, well I can only say she'd wrote some *epics*.

'Come *on*!' goes Ol, screwing up his programme. 'Finish it off, will yer?'

The poet announces yet another one.

'Oh *no*!' says Ol. 'Give in, will yer?'

Applause. The curtain starts to fall.

'Do anuvver one!' goes Ol. 'Encore! Encore!'

Out in the hall we can hear them all traipsing off for tea and fairy cakes. They'll be back in ten minutes, and waiting for us.

'Let's go,' says Gail, grabbing her bass drum. 'Come on, everyone! Let's go!'

We move on to the stage, dragging the gear with us. Wingnut searches for a lead, and Ol struggles with a gym ramp that's been left. But it's not really happening, not *really*. I set out the mikes, like I been told – one by the bass drum, two over the kit, one by Ol's amp, one by Wingnut's, and one out front for the vocals. It's as if I'm watching someone else doing it.

'They're comin' back!' says Ol. 'Where's *Reaney*? 'Elp me wiv this ramp, someone!'

There's a bunch of kids appeared offstage.

'Oy!' I shout at them. 'Get this ramp off, will yer?'

A couple of the kids wander on. They ain't bothered none. They're more interested in the little conversation they're having. I shout at them again, and they bend down, dead lazy, and take hold of the ramp.

'Lost yer singer then?' says this red-haired kid.

''Ow d'you know about it?' I go.

They drag the ramp past me and off the side of the stage. 'Been suspended, ain't 'e?' says the red-haired kid.

'What?'

Ol drops his lead and bursts across the stage. Next second, the kid's pinned against the p.a. speakers, with a fist under his chin.

'What you talkin' about?' says Ol. 'What you sayin' 'bout Yatesy?'

''Ang on!' goes the kid. 'Dontcha know about it?'

'Course I don't bloody know, or I wouldn't be askin', would I?' says Ol.

'No need to swear.'

'*Tell* me!' Ol grabs the kid's arm and wrenches it behind his back. The rest of us crowd round.

'All right!' goes the kid. 'Leave off, will yer? I'll tell yer!'

Ol relaxes, just a bit.

''Appened last lesson, didn't it?' says the kid. 'Whole crowd of 'em been after 'im for ages, right? They see 'is class muckin' about in the Drama room – no teacher around. So they go in there, don't they? They push him about a bit. 'E don't fight back, so they try to get 'im needled. They 'as a go at his face, an' 'is clothes. They call 'im chicken. An' then one o' them says 'e comes out o' the gutter. All of a sudden, 'e throws a wobbler. 'E goes *right off his head*. Ga, you shoulda seen the way 'e smacked this kid! 'E put 'im clean out, didn't 'e? 'E would've put the lot out an' all, if the whole crowd hadn't sat on 'im. Blood everywhere, there was! An' the kid 'e smacked's in 'ospital! Evans did 'is nut. 'E suspended Yatesy straight off. 'E's still in Evans's room now, while they try an' get 'is old man in.'

'It wasn't 'is fault!' shouts Olly.

'All right!' says the kid. 'Lay off, will yer? Ain't you on now?'

Ol lets go, and stares round himself like he don't know where he is.

'Funny thin' is,' says the kid, 'Yatesy's class 'ad a teacher all the time! They was in the middle of a lesson!'

'What?'

The kid cracks into an ugly great smile. 'Dreamy Reaney!' he goes.

We ain't nothing but open mouths. Out in the hall, the audience has gone all quiet.

'On the mixer, Bill,' says Ol. 'C'mon you lot – let's go.'

The band run out on to the stage. I'm so scared, I'm crippled. But I squeeze past the speakers, and out round the edge of the curtain.

'Urrray!'

It's OK. I'm invisible. Tell you, miss – not even me dad can see me. It ain't me the morons are trying to trip up. There's only one thing in this hall, and that's our mixer. And it's getting closer. It's getting closer. I'm there. I stare down at that massive bank of controls, and now I flip. Which one's the bloody on-switch?

Why are they stamping their feet?

Ah. It's coming back to me. Yes, that's the one, I'm sure of it. I reach for the little red switch, and I flick it down. A filthy great wail of feedback comes screaming out of the speakers, and every pair of hands in the hall flashes up over ears.

Miss, I'm that close to running, me trainers are already on their way. But just then, God sends me a third hand. It creeps up beside the other two, and pulls down a slider. The noise stops.

The hand's Reaney's.

'Sir!' I go. 'What 'bout your lesson?'

'Signal the curtains, will you?' says Reaney. 'Sorry, I just got back from the hospital.'

I wave. There's a moronic cheer. The curtain crawls open, and Gail, Wingnut and Olly blink into the light.

'Let's give it some, shall we?' says Reaney. He pushes

the slider marked master volume, and ups the bass all round.

The band still ain't started. Ol stares out, all mad and confused, but he don't count them in. I see Reaney's fingers cross.

Ol taps the mike. 'One two,' he goes.

'Three four!' go the audience.

Ol turns towards the others, and forgets he's by the mike. 'Count of four, right?' he goes.

'One, two, three, *four*!' go the audience.

Disaster. Gail comes in. Ol and Wingnut don't. The crowd love it. They join in with the drums, clapping and stamping their feet. Ol waves his arms about, but he can't cut it out. Teachers pop up and down like ducks on a shooting gallery.

I could cry. There's Ol and Wingers stood up there with their arms folded, while Gail thrashes on for all she's worth, and the audience makes all the noise!

'Come on,' says Reaney. 'Just –'

I don't hear no more. All of a sudden there's this massive roar from the crowd. Something's going on out there. I jump to me feet, but so do half the kids in the hall. It's over by the door, whatever it is. No it ain't – it's at the front. Or is it on stage?

It's the voice I hear first. It's like a smack in the face. Yatesy! He's on the mike!

For once, there's no need for arguing. The band chuck all the plans out the window, and go straight into the rap. Only it ain't that weedy thrash from the practice room. It comes out them speakers like a *train*. Right, and tight. Right, and tight, and with that much balls it's *criminal*. They can hardly believe it's them that's doing it.

> 'I can't sing over this!
> I just *can't* sing over this!'

Yatesy springs around the stage, slippery, scarey, like a touched frog. He levels his finger at the crowd, jabbing and jabbing, while the words come pouring out of him, like a flurry of punches. Everything that lot's flung at him's coming right back in their faces. He tells the teachers, and the kids cheer their heads off. Then he tells the kids, and they still cheer. Crying out he is, like a wounded animal, with moans and growls, and all the words they won't let us use.

> 'I can't sing over this, can I?
> I *can't* sing over this, can I?'

Yatesy's loose arm whirrs away behind him, winding up the band, driving them as mad as he is. They're just one voice now, one brain, one single purpose. As the chorus comes round again, Ol jumps up next to Yatesy and joins in. In seconds, the crowd's chanting along. Some of them start to tramp their feet and punch the air. It's like we're in a giant pressure cooker, all set to blow apart.

> 'I can't . . . I can't . . . I can't . . .'

I'm scared. I don't know what's what any more. Who they are, who I am, what we're all doing here. Down at the front, Hatton's on his feet. A cake flies out of nowhere and hits him round the ear. Then silence.

Someone's pulled the plugs on us.

The crowd whistles. Ol chucks down his guitar in disgust. Yatesy just carries right on, but all he is is a hoarse shout in the distance. Up on stage comes Disco, to take the mike away. 'Ladies and gentlemen!' he calls out. 'Let's not get carried away, *please*!'

Out in the hall, Hatton singles out some kid and smacks him round the leg, two, three times. The crowd simmers down to a murmur, and Disco turns to the band. 'Come on, lads,' he says. 'You've had your say.' He takes hold of Olly's arm, and Ol jerks it away. Two more teachers get up on stage and grab Yatesy, even though he's gone limp as a pile of rags.

I look round at Reaney. His hands are still there on the controls, and his eyes are brimming with tears.

7

I suppose you'll be wondering if the show got finished OK, miss. Well, it did. That's to say, acts got on stage, the parents clapped, the crawlers laughed, and the teachers sat on the ends of all the rows. Cinderella was off to the ball again, and Yatesy's rap had never happened.

We were dead men, and we knew it. We'd cop it from school, and we'd cop it at home. But that wasn't the worst feeling. We were so stirred up, you know? Something ought to be *happening*. There should be something to *do*, somewhere to *go*. But all we'd got was the packing up.

So we packed up. We lifted off the speakers, rolled up the leads, and put the amps, drums and guitars in their cases. A few kids come over and told us they were setting up bands next year. I don't know what they expected us to say. But they helped out, so that was something.

Reaney seemed to understand what we were going through. He told us it was natural to feel let down after a gig. And sometimes, he said, after the best gigs, it was the worst feeling. As we loaded the last of the gear into the van, I asked him about his lesson. He said it was best forgot, like his teaching career. 'Probably a good thing in the long run,' he said.

Ol's sat on the steps nearby, tuning in. 'It's our fault,' he goes. 'We dragged you into it. *I* dragged you into it.'

Reaney squats next to him, and looks him in the eyes. 'Listen,' he says. 'Let's get this straight. I *wanted* to help you. And you've more than paid me for it.'

Ol checks him. He means it. The others come over, and we talk about Yatesy's rap instead. All the band reckon it lasted about twenty seconds. We tell them it was at least three minutes, but they still won't have it.

'That boy 'e 'it all right, sir?' says Gail.

'Just concussion,' says Reaney. 'He's all right.'

'Ga!' I go. ''E must've really smacked 'im one!'

Ol nudges me in the ribs. I look up. Yatesy's stood by the van, watching us.

'All right?' goes Olly.

'All right,' says Yatesy.

No one knows what to say. Except Winston, that is. He wants his petrol money. Reaney says it's his treat, pays him, and shakes hands. The van's jammed to the roof, and there's no way any of us are getting a lift home. So we all say thanks to Winston, who never got nothing from helping us, and give him directions out.

'Let's all walk,' says Gail.

'Where?' I go.

'Let's just walk.'

The rain's stopped now, and left everything smelling all earthy and ready. We set off down the gravel path through the copse. Mr Reaney wanders off in front, talking keyboards with Wingnut. Gail's next, trying to get some words out of Yatesy. Ol and me back up the rear, crunching the gravel in time. 'See yer old man?' says Ol.

'Nah.'

'Maybe he wasn't there.'

'I 'ope 'e was.'

Ol's surprised. Then he nods, and grins. 'Ey, Gail!' he shouts. 'Can me an' Bill come an' live round yours?'

Gail's more concerned with Yatesy. When we catch them up, we find out exactly what we already knew. Yatesy's been kicked out. Haley Comp. was just another school to Yatesy, but what bothers him is his old man, and how he's going to take the news.

'We'll all go round,' says Gail. 'We'll tell your dad they should've kept you, an' expelled the *school*. Won't we, Bill? Won't we, Ol?'

We say we will. Yatesy cheers up a bit on that score, but something's still bugging him.

The path runs out of the copse, and down one side of that new Youth Training Centre. Then we come out on the common, and suddenly there's space in front of us, years and years of it. Too much for Ol, it is. He's off hunting the buffalo. Then he's dribbling through the Brazil defence, and putting a fir cone into orbit. Goal! he shouts. Offside! I shout back. Ref! he shouts, dropping on to his knees.

Something's up. He don't get to his feet. He just stays there, curled up, and dead still.

'You all right, Ol?'

Really, really slow, his head uncurls.

'Listen,' he goes.

We stop. 'Can't 'ear nuffing,' I go.

'You're not *listening*,' goes Ol.

We try again. And this time, we start to hear it. Way, way off, over the other side of the copse. The voices are faint, but they're *there* . . . and there's no way we can mistake what they're chanting.

'I can't sing over this, can I?
I *can't* sing over this, can I?'

We're struck dumb. *Struck dumb*. Ol's face is all stretched out and amazed, with huge eyes. His fists start to tighten up, till his arms tremble, and then every inch of him.

'We . . . *done* it,' he goes. 'We done it! We done it!'

He flies into the air, like a rocket. He hugs Gail. He slaps my hand. He kisses Wingnut. And then we're all doing it. We're hugging and patting and bouncing round the common like a bunch of loonies.

'We showed 'em!' goes Ol. 'We showed them teachers!'

'An' my old man!' I go.

'An' all them boys!' goes Gail.

'An' . . . an' . . . everyone!' goes Ol. 'Didn't we, sir?'

'You showed *yourselves*,' says Reaney.

'Yeah, we showed us!' goes Ol. 'We showed us all right!'

Ol races round and pulls us all down, before someone does themselves an injury. 'Let's do somefing!' he goes. 'Let's celebrate!'

'What we gonna do, Mr Reaney?' says Gail.

'Oh, I wouldn't ask me,' says Reaney. 'Not after my disaster today.'

'That's it!' goes Ol. 'Let's do your disaster, sir!'

'What – here?' says Reaney.

You can see his point. There we are, in the middle of nowhere, in the middle of the night. A bunch of troublemakers and a kicked-out teacher.

'Why not?' says Ol. 'Come on, you old 'ippy!'

Reaney looks round and reads our faces. Then he claps his hands, takes hold of our shoulders, and moves us into a circle. 'Volunteer?'

Ol steps forward, into the centre of the circle. ''Ere,' he goes. 'You can all get yer own back on me.'

Reaney asks Olly to close his eyes, and the rest of us to get closer together. In a moment, Olly's going to completely relax – and just fall. Whoever he falls to has got to take the weight, and push him off again. Someone else catches him, and so on. But it won't work less we all concentrate, and Ol lets go completely.

One of Ol's eyes peeps open. Ready? he says. Right, we go. Ready? he says. Right, we go.

'Ready?'

'Right!'

Ol falls, like a chimney, right on me. He weighs a ton, but I bear up OK, and lever him over to Gail. She pushes him right across the circle to Yatesy. Suddenly Ol decides this is a good laugh, and next time I get him, he's just like a sack of feathers. And when we tell him his time's up and stand him in the middle, he goes One More Time! and drops again. Reaney's got to dive like Peter Shilton to save him.

Course, everyone's keen now. Wingers spends the whole time squealing like a piglet, then asks for another go. Gail takes it dead serious, but ends up laughing her head off. Poor old Reaney's a bit too big, so that makes it Yatesy's turn.

Yatesy shuffles into the middle, scratching at his straw hair. For a moment his eyes close. Then he's shaking his head, shaking and shaking it. 'What's up, Yatesy?' goes Gail. 'Don't yer trust us?'

'I ain't yer friend,' says Yatesy. 'I ain't one of yer.'

'What d'yer mean?' we all go.

'Well . . . this was it, wasn't it?' says Yatesy. 'This was the night. Now it's finished, ain't it – the group.'

Everyone looks at Olly. 'What yer staring at me for?' says Ol. '*Four* people in this band, y'know!'

Old Yatesy can't seem to grasp how come we're all laughing.

'Come on, Yatesy!' says Ol, poking him on the arm. 'You ain't chickenin' out the band *again*, are yer?'

Yatesy checks we all think the same. Then he closes his eyes. Then he drops.

Needless to say, I got my go in the end, miss. It was a weird feeling. It reminded me of when I was dead little, and me dad used to chuck me up and down. I never thought I'd get hurt or nothing. I just trusted him, like you trusted us, and we let you down.

Well, that's about it, I suppose. It ain't really an ending, but if you has endings, there ain't nothing left to happen, is there? You know miss, what bugs me about writing is that no matter how hard you try, it ain't life, or even a patch on it. Still, I hope I ain't bored you, cos there's nothing worse than being bored.

Now miss, you got to promise me two things. First, you got to write and tell us everything that's happened to you in China. And second, when you come back, you got to get all your mates together, and come to see a band called the Steady Circle.

Other books in this series

MAX ON EARTH
Marilyn Kaye

The first of four books about strange, golden-haired Max, an alien from another world who has come to Earth to learn how to behave in a human manner and picks on Randi Hill to help her. With a bit of camouflage, they make her look fairly normal. She learns quickly and makes friends, but when it comes to understanding human emotions poor Max is at a loss – what on earth makes Randi behave the way she does when handsome, athletic Gary is around?

OF GRIFFINS AND GRAFFITI
Kate Gilmore

It was an ordinary boring Saturday evening when the idea of doing a really special piece of graffiti came to Steven Wiley and his friends. But *how?*, *when?* and *where?* were the questions. Then Steve came up with a terrific idea. A fast-paced, topical and very funny story, set in the New York of the eighties. The author, a native New Yorker, has captured the exciting and dangerous world of the graffiti artist in a way that makes this a gripping and unputdownable read.

KILL-A-LOUSE WEEK AND OTHER STORIES
Susan Gregory

The new head arrives at Davenport Secondary just as the 'Kill-a-Louse' campaign is starting. Soon the whole school is in uproar – can it be that rebellion is as catching as nits in the hair? These thirteen stories introduce a lively collection of school characters.

THE BEST LITTLE GIRL IN THE WORLD

Steven Levenkron

Francesca is five feet four, pretty, slim and intelligent – at least that's how she appears to the rest of the world. But what she sees when she looks at her reflection is a fat, flabby, grotesque monster. Suddenly, meals become dangerous to her. Food is the enemy and must be beaten! And what starts as determination soon becomes a frightening obsession – anorexia nervosa – with everyone realizing that her life is in danger . . .

THE DAY THEY CAME TO ARREST THE BOOK

Nat Hentoff

Whoever heard of a literary classic being banned from school? Well, that's just what happens at the George Mason High School, when a small group of parents and students brand *Huckleberry Finn* as racist, sexist and immoral, and persuade the principal to remove it from the library shelves. There is plenty to agree and disagree with in this provocative and witty portrait of a community in conflict.

LOCKED IN TIME

Lois Duncan

When seventeen-year-old Nore Robbins arrives at the old Louisiana plantation home of her father and his new wife, she is prepared for unhappiness. She did not expect her new family to be so *different*, nor can she understand her own mixed-up feelings about them. As time passes she pieces together a strange and terrible truth about the family; Nore alone is a threat to their secret – and threats must be destroyed.

UNEASY MONEY

Robin F. Brancato

What would *you* do if you won a fortune? That's what happened to Mike Bronti when he bought a New Jersey lottery ticket. Suddenly everything looks possible: gifts for his family, treats for his friends, a new car for himself – but things don't work out quite as he expects. He soon finds out that money can bring problems and unhappiness, and what started out as a happy spending spree soon turns into a frantic effort to win back his father's respect.

THE TRICKSTERS

Margaret Mahy

The Hamiltons gather at their holiday house for their usual celebration of midsummer Christmas in New Zealand, but the warm, chaotic family atmosphere is chilled by the unexpected arrrival of three sinister brothers – the Tricksters. Who are they? Where are they from? Only Harry, the middle daughter, is close to seeing the truth, but even she is unsure. Are these brothers her own invention or the embodiment of Teddy Carnival who is thought to have drowned here many years ago?

BREAKING GLASS

Brian Morse

When the Red Army drops its germ bomb on Leicester, the Affected Zone is sealed off permanently – with Darren and his sister Sally inside it. Immune to the disease which kills Sally, Darren must face alone the incomprehensible hatred of Alex and Budge, two other survivors trapped with him. And forever haunting him is the question: Why did Dad not come back for them?